# The Great Houdinis!

# The Great Houdinis!

## A Vaudeville

by

**Melville Shavelson**

A FAWCETT CREST BOOK

Fawcett Publications, Inc., Greenwich, Connecticut

Lines from "C.L.M." reprinted with permission of
Macmillan Publishing Co., Inc., from *Poems* by
John Masefield. Copyright 1912 by Macmillan Publishing
Co., Inc., renewed 1940 by John Masefield.

*THE GREAT HOUDINIS!*

A Fawcett Crest Original

ISBN: 0-449-23043-0

Printed in the United States of America

10   9   8   7   6   5   4   3   2   1

*In the dark womb where I began*
*My mother's life made me a man.*
*Through all the months of human birth*
*Her beauty fed my common earth.*
*I cannot see, nor breathe, nor stir,*
*But through the death of some of her.*

—fragment of John Masefield's *C.L.M.*,
found in Houdini's diary after his death

*His career spanned the life of that other phenomenon, vaudeville, which was born in that other century, too, and passed away almost at the moment Harry did, with the advent of radio and the talking moving picture, poor substitutes for flesh and blood. For over thirty years, vaudeville was the lifeblood of entertainment in the United States and Europe. In its comics and its tragedians, its song-and-dance men and its acrobats, its lovely ladies and its gaudy magicians, vaudeville ran the gamut of human emotion in performances that always began with an overture and finished with an afterpiece.*

*The orchestra is striking up. The candy butchers are falling silent.*

*Curtain going up.*

## OVERTURE

~~~~~~~~~~~~~~~~~

THE Woolworth Building was the tallest building in New York at the time. It towered above Manhattan, a building built on nickels and dimes in a day when nickels and dimes could buy anything, including the newspapers that had to have a sensation a day to endure. The *World*, the *Graphic*, the *Journal*, with their stories of sugar daddies and chorus girls and rum runners and G-men. Two centes daily, five cents for the Sunday edition.

They were all on that tugboat, the newspapers' cynical reporters and O. O. McIntyre and Ray Jaure, the *Graphic*'s leading sob sister, and from New York Harbor the Woolworth Building was visible, a symbol of man's aspiration and the heights it could achieve. Certainly no one would ever get closer to heaven.

On the deck a man named Ehrich Weiss, his
hands and feet manacled, was placed in a huge
packing box. He wore only a one-piece bathing
suit, a ridiculous thing that came to his knees,
but he would willingly have gone into the box
naked. That would have eliminated the photographers, though, and they were important; the *World*
and the *Graphic* and the *Journal* were what made
Ehrich Weiss the Great Houdini.

The tugboat made its way to the middle of the
harbor and the packing box was nailed shut by
the reporters themselves.

From the upper deck, a small, dark-haired
woman watched. She was in her forties then, beautiful, frail, but with an inner strength that could
move mountains—and had. Although she knew
this was a show, fear touched her, not so much
for the obvious peril of the moment, but for what
had become of the man she loved. This moment
was unnecessary; he was already a long-established
success. Why risk death for the newspapers and
a few added dollars at the box office on Broadway?

Why? What was he searching for? His mother?
The mother who had called him *meshugeneh*?
Ehrich, why must you always do crazy things? Why
should you try you should kill yourself twice a
day, three times on *Shabbas*?

The packing case with Ehrich Weiss inside was
lifted by a huge cargo hook and placed on a chute.

Then suddenly it was released, and slid down over the side and splashed into the icy waters of the harbor. Weighted down by lead weights lashed to its planks, it sank like a stone into the depths, and the vaudeville had begun.

For this was before the human image was put into cans and onto magnetic tape in wholesale lots. The performers came right to your own home town, and you could see them eating in the restaurants and walking down Main Street and, quite often, dating your girl, before you put down your quarter and walked into the Bijou or the Strand to watch the lights go down and see the spotlight come up and change them into gods. Or flops. And that was part of the thrill. They knew. They knew immediately how you felt about them, and they reacted to it, because they were right there in front of you, and how you booed or applauded affected what they did. The audience was the most important part of vaudeville, and that was Harry Houdini's secret—not the trick escapes and the gimmicked props of his imitators, but the fact that he knew how to make the audience feel he was going to die.

That's why they all came, to see Houdini die. There's no record of how the audience that finally saw him do it reacted. They probably applauded.

At that moment in New York Harbor, the audience was the *World* and the *Graphic* and the *Journal*, and at first they reacted cynically—another stunt to grab some free space—but after a while, when Harry didn't come up out of the depths of New York Harbor, they began to worry, individually, as human beings, not newspapermen. They didn't want their companions to see they were worried, because it was, after all, just part of the act. And still he didn't come up. And still. And still. And suddenly it was no longer a story in the newspapers. It was happening. No human being could last that long without oxygen. And they started shouting for someone to help him, to dive in and find him, at the same time that they were seeing their bylines: HOUDINI DROWNS! By O. O. McIntyre.

And just at that moment, he shot to the surface, triumphantly waving his chains above his head, panting for breath, smiling for the photographers, the string having been drawn as taut as it could stretch. You could almost hear the vaudeville pit band striking up a fanfare, the cymbals shimmering on top of the percussion, and only Bess Houdini, her knuckles white from gripping the railing, knew what the music celebrated. Death had only taken a holiday.

Mama would have to wait until Halloween.

*Rosabelle, sweet Rosabelle,*
*I love you more than I can tell. . . .*

⌇⌇⌇⌇⌇⌇⌇⌇⌇⌇⌇⌇⌇⌇⌇⌇⌇⌇⌇⌇⌇⌇⌇⌇⌇⌇⌇⌇⌇⌇⌇⌇⌇⌇⌇⌇⌇⌇⌇⌇⌇⌇⌇

# ACT ONE

MACHPELACH Cemetery in Queens is as crowded as the tenements of Ehrich Weiss's youth. Tombstone crouches over tombstone, only yards away from the noise and fumes of a busy metropolitan highway.

It was cold that day, that day in the fall of 1928, a very good year unless you were dead. Lindy had flown the Atlantic the year before, Babe Ruth had hit his sixtieth home run, *Show Boat* had opened, the first Mickey Mouse cartoon had appeared, Wall Street had hit a peak, and Sacco and Vanzetti had been executed. A very good year.

And it was Halloween, the second anniversary of the first time Harry Houdini had failed to get out of a coffin.

Two women walked along the pathway between

the crowded headstones, the wind blowing the leaves about their feet, rain dripping from the trees, a damp chill adding to the gloom. One of the women was Bess Houdini, older now, but still Bess. Sadness had touched but not crushed her. She wore a cloth coat bundled about her, a scarf knotted firmly at her neck, a hat and gloves, and in her hand she carried a small cluster of roses, out of place here, because this was an Orthodox Jewish cemetery where the customary offering is a pebble. But Harry Houdini was no ordinary tenant, and even after his death he was treated as a headliner; whatever he wanted backstage was okay with the management.

Beside Bess walked her companion and nurse, Minnie Chester, a tough, middle-aged New Yorker, an ex-vaudevillian herself, dressed in the worst possible taste and proud of it. She watched her patient with a professional eye, and what she saw disturbed her. Bess's face was white; she coughed occasionally and tightened the scarf about her neck.

"I gotta be outa my mind," Minnie told her. "Two days out of the hospital, I should never have let you come here in this weather."

"I'm all right."

"That's what they all thought. It would keep a lot of doctors on their toes if *their* names hadda be carved into the tombstones, too." She shivered. "Brrr. I wanna be cremated. I'll stay warm longer."

Bess hadn't heard. She had paused, as she always did. Only Harry could have managed it. Here, in the heart of Orthodoxy, a carved marble bust atop his ornate monument. "Thou shalt make no graven images," Jehovah had commanded the faithful, and his word had been followed by all those who rested at Machpelach. All except Harry Houdini, who had designed his own final resting place. He had even had himself photographed on it while it was under construction. He had decided there would be a marble bust of himself, and with a little sleight of hand, Jehovah had somehow been hoodwinked. You had the feeling He somehow enjoyed it, as all of Harry's audiences enjoyed being fooled, because it had been done so well. In the winter, when the snow sometimes drifted high enough to cover all the other tombstones, all that was visible above the mantle of white was the lonely marble face of Harry Houdini, proudly surveying the graveyard where, as in life, he had eliminated all competition. And when the thaws came and the snows melted, they revealed, carved in stone, kneeling in grief at his monument, Our Lady of Sorrows, who had managed to slip over from some Gentile cemetery unnoticed, at Harry's bidding. Above her, in red and gold—the only spot of color allowed among all of the Orthodox headstones—was the emblem of the Society of American Magicians, Harry Houdini, President.

Magician indeed. It took the weight of the entire

monument to keep his father, Rabbi Maier Weiss, buried on Harry's right, from getting up and walking out.

But it was the grave on his left that Bess was looking at. She knew the inscription by heart: "Here In Eternal Peace Lies Our Darling Mother."

"There he is," Bess sighed, "right next to Mama. She's got him all to herself at last. After all these years she's finally—"

She stopped, abruptly. Someone who had been kneeling beside the gravesite had slowly risen into view. It was a woman, dressed simply but theatrically, young and pretty in the Broadway sense, obviously a little embarrassed to have been discovered here, but enough of an actress to cover it up.

"Hello, Bess," she said quietly. Daisy White had played the Keith-Albee Circuit as a magician's assistant. She knew very well when it was time to disappear.

"Hello, Daisy," Bess said, and suddenly it was very cold in the cemetery, colder than it had been before.

"This place is starting to look like his dressing room." Minnie had little regard for diplomacy.

Daisy took the hint. "Well," she said, "I got to get back to the city, I got a matinee."

"Anyone we know?" Bess inquired sweetly.

And the moment was over. Daisy turned without a word and walked away, between the rows of silent headstones engraved with the Star of David.

Minnie took Bess's arm. "You're not as sick as you look," she said approvingly, steering her toward the monument. "That was a lesson in how to saw a woman in half."

"Minnie . . . could you let me be here . . . alone . . . for a few minutes?"

Minnie looked at her face, and understood.

"Okay. I'll go windowshop."

She moved off. Bess crossed to the ornate stone and dropped to her knees. She saw the roses Daisy had left, picked them up and threw them to one side, and put her own in their place. And then she looked up at the marble bust that seemed to be watching from above.

"Hello, Harry, you son of a bitch," she said.

"Bess! Bess! Come here!"

She looked off, and Harry was calling to her from among the headstones in the sunlight and amid the blossoms of that spring day in St. Joe, Missouri, so long ago, in that other century, in that other cemetery, and for a moment she was young again, and frightened, and following after him with the pad and pencil in her hand, as he ran, searching, from one grave to another, until he found the one he was looking for.

"James Oliver Fitzpatrick, Born 1822, Died 1893. 'He Lives in My Heart.' Loving wife. Colleen."

Bess knelt beside him.

"Harry, we shouldn't be doing this."

"Copy it down, it's the mayor's uncle."

After all, he was her husband, even if it had only been for a few months, so she tried to obey, something young wives used to do in those distant times.

"It's insane," she said. "We don't know how to hold a seance; they'll find out right away."

"I'll do the voices, you pass the hat."

"Couldn't we just do the magic act?"

"It's been laying an egg in every dime museum and tent show from here to Chicago. We've had two weeks canceled, we owe for the hotel, I hadda cash in the train tickets, you think I wanna stay in St. Joe for the rest of my life?" Harry indicated the other headstones. "They hadda put rocks on their chests to keep *them* here."

"Harry, I can't." She held out her hand for him to see, a small hand trembling so it could barely hold the pencil. He looked at her for a moment, and the look softened. He took her hand in his and kissed it.

"You're absolutely beautiful when you're scared."

She looked at him, startled. She was a very young bride, they were in love and free with each other in bed, sometimes out of it, but this was different. He pulled her to him and kissed her, but she pushed him away.

"Holy Mother of God! Not here!"

"Why the hell not here?" He kissed her again.

"Everybody's dead!"

*"We're* not. Death is the only enemy, you know that? We have to show him life is stronger than he is."

She felt the strength in his arms as he forced her down to the ground between the tombstones, the strength of the body that had been trained to escape from all restraints, imprisoning her own now. Her struggling became weaker, there was no denying the excitement of being taken in a place like this, a place like this at high noon, and all she could manage to say was, "Harry! This is my only good skirt!"

"I'm giving her philosophy, she's giving me dry goods."

He kissed her again, forcing her body down into the yielding grass. His hands were inside her dress now, flesh was touching flesh, and it was true, this was life, this was the living defying the death that was all around them.

She felt him within her.

"Harry," she whispered, "we're desecrating holy ground."

"It's all right, it's all right. My father was a rabbi."

They disappeared from sight behind the headstones. The breeze continued to blow, scattering the blossoms from the branches. . . .

"Mrs. Houdini?"

Bess looked up, startled, blushing, catching her-

self as she realized it had been only a memory.
She was kneeling in front of Harry's grave in
Queens, New York, and she could hear the traffic
rolling by on the highway nearby, a long way from
St. Joe, from 1895.

It was a voice she had never heard before. She
turned her head and saw a pair of shoes, new and
highly polished. She looked up, and there was a
figure towering over her, a figure in a dark overcoat with an alpaca collar, a walking stick in his
hand, and the turned collar of a minister. At
Machpelach Orthodox Cemetery.

Slowly, she rose to her feet, and turned to face
him.

"Yes?"

"I wouldn't intrude at a moment like this, but
it's important."

He was a young man. She had never thought of
anyone wearing the collar as being young and
good-looking and speaking with a Southern accent;
it gave an unreal flavor to the moment.

"Who are you? How did you know I was here?"

"I went to your house, and the maid told me."

Minnie had hurried to them, puzzled, worried.

"That was the cleaning lady," she told him. "I'm
the maid, the companion, the nurse. I also juggle
and whistle Dixie."

"Minnie, shhh!" Bess turned to the young man
again. "Do I know you?"

"I don't think so. I'm the Reverend Arthur Ford,

Rector of the First Spiritualist Church of New York."

"Oy vay," said Minnie.

"I'm sorry, don't you read the papers?" said Bess. "I've withdrawn the offer."

Bess turned away and took Minnie's arm, the meeting over as far as she was concerned. The money that she had posted for anyone who could bring her a message from beyond the grave, over the past two years, had proved an embarrassing exposure of human nature at its worst.

Reverend Ford was following them.

"I'm not interested in the $10,000."

"Shall I whistle Dixie?" asked Minnie.

"Reverend Ford." Bess turned, a little sadly, because she had thought him a nice young man. "In the two years since Harry died, I've been convinced he was right: all of the people who claim to communicate with the Hereafter are either crooks or lunatics."

"Take your choice, Reverend," Minnie said. "Personally, I don't think you're a lunatic."

She led Bess toward the entrance to the cemetery, passing through the archway to the side of the highway, where the traffic continued to flow, the Reos and the Franklins and the Packards.

Ford followed, his manner polite, his voice sincere. "I practice a religion, not a fraud, Mrs. Houdini. Someone is trying to contact you from the Beyond, through me."

"Oh, come on, Reverend. Harry and I used to do that in the act."

"And badly, too," added Minnie. "Nice to have met you." And she waved for a taxi, which pulled up to the curb. Minnie opened the door, and Bess started to get in.

"Does the name 'Cecilia' mean anything to you?"

Bess stopped. For a fraction of a second she hesitated, then she turned back.

"Mrs. Weiss? Harry's mother?"

"Yes."

"Excuse me, Reverend, I never cared to hear from the old *yenta* when she was alive, I certainly don't intend to listen to her when she's dead." She coughed again. "Come on, Minnie, let's go home. I'm getting cold."

They got into the cab. Minnie paused to lean out and wave goodbye.

"If you hear from Robert E. Lee," she called, "tell him he lost."

She rolled up the window.

He stood there, quietly, helplessly, watching them go. Then he turned and started away.

As Bess looked back through the rear window of the taxi, she thought she saw a woman, who had been standing near the cemetery entrance, turn to follow him.

She might have been Daisy White.

The rain beat against the window pane, making

little crooked streams down the surface, distorting
the images of the jack o'lanterns in the windows
across the street, real pumpkins with real candles
in them, none of your papier-mâché imitations in
those days. Thunder rumbled in the distance, un-
seasonal thunder. It was a night for birds to walk
and witches to ride, Bess thought, as she sat on
the couch, feeling miserable, letting Minnie pour
the cough medicine. The living room was almost
as Harry had left it—the ornate furnishings, the
heavy wallpaper, the deep rugs, the lamps that
shed little light. Not many people knew that the
room had been gimmicked, little secret panels in
the arms of the chairs, glasses that had tiny mirrors
set inside them so objects could be hidden when
the glass appeared full of water. The Great Houdini
must never be at a loss when visitors demanded
to see some little unrehearsed trick. And Harry,
grinning to himself, enjoyed their amazement at
his powers. Sir Arthur Conan Doyle himself had
testified in public that he had stood beside Houdini
on the stage when he performed his famous illusion
of walking through a solid brick wall, and had felt
Harry dematerialize his body and materialize it
on the other side. Nothing Harry could say short
of exposing the simple trap that made it all possible
would convince his British friend, and Harry wasn't
going to expose a trick that helped earn $3,000 a
week. What made him more angry was the testimony of the spiritualists that Houdini obviously

had psychic powers, that he was concealing from the public that his tricks were performed by supernatural means, that perhaps he himself didn't realize he was being assisted from the Beyond. His answer to all that was, simply, "Horse manure."

The thunder rumbled again. Bess couldn't help remembering, although she tried not to, why they had stopped doing their seances onstage. Harry had seen a little boy riding a bicycle outside the theater, his mother watching proudly, and when later the mother came up on the stage, Harry had pretended to look into the future and told her her little boy was going to break his right arm.

He was dumfounded the next day when the mother called him, in tears, to accuse him of black magic. Her boy had fallen from his bicycle that night and his right arm had been broken. Harry immediately canceled the next performance, although he knew it had to be coincidence. But he never held another seance, except to expose their practitioners. And he never spoke about the incident, or allowed Bess to speak of it. She felt, in her heart, that Harry knew there was something strange about himself that he couldn't fathom, and it frightened him.

His photo stared down at her from above the mantel, beside the picture of Mama in a gold frame. Bess tried to take her mind off it. But it was Halloween night, the anniversary of his death, the time they had both agreed she would concentrate on his picture, and that he would find some means of getting through to her, if anyone could, some time, some way, some Halloween night in the future.

She turned to Minnie, trying to forget.

"Do you think he was a real minister?" she asked. They had been speaking of Arthur Ford.

"Why not? I am. Remember, Harry once had me ordained by mail order." Minnie had poured the cough medicine into a spoon. "Of course, what I really wanna be is a witch doctor, but you have to go to school for that. Open."

Bess made a face, like a child, as the bitter medicine burned her throat. That's how you knew it was working, in those direct days, if it burned your throat. Doctors made house calls, medicine burned your throat, iodine tortured germs to death; only a few people believed you could cure anything with medicine that tasted good or by lying on a couch and talking about your mother.

"Horrible medicine. Tastes like bootleg hooch."

"Next time I'll put an olive in it," Minnie said, as she got to her feet. "I'll make you some more tea."

"On your way, straighten Mama's picture."

Minnie stopped and looked at the portrait of Cecilia Weiss, hanging over the mantel beside Bess's favorite photograph of Harry, with the *Yortzeit* candle beneath it, the candle that burned from sundown to sundown in mourning. Mama's picture was hanging slightly askew, staring quizzically at

Minnie, the hint of a smile on the wise lips, in the old-fashioned lace-collared dress. The Orthodox Mona Lisa.

"I could have sworn I straightened it when I came in," Minnie said thoughtfully. Thunder rolled again, in the distance. Perhaps that had done it. Minnie shrugged, crossed to Mama, and straightened the portrait.

"Why do you keep it hanging?"

"I promised Harry."

"You think he'll know?"

"Would you bet against him?"

Minnie shrugged and picked up the tea tray. "It's two years, he hasn't made it back, and he wasn't even handcuffed this time."

"Maybe Harry doesn't think it's enough of a challenge," Bess said, and smiled. She lay back on the sofa.

There was a loud rapping at the front door. Then, just as suddenly, silence.

"Now, who's that at this hour?" Minnie grumbled, as she crossed and opened it. She looked out. Rain spattered the empty street, blown by the wind, reflecting the grinning face of the jack o'lantern across the pavement. Minnie shivered from the cold, and closed the door.

"Halloween," she decided, heading for the kitchen. "Those goddam kids." And she slammed the door behind her.

Thunder, in the distance, hollow-sounding,

strange. Slowly, Bess sat bolt upright on the sofa. Mama's picture was hanging at an angle again, the Mona Lisa cocking her head as if asking her if she had seen how it had been done.

A hollow rapping at the door again. Bess started, involuntarily.

"Minnie!"

No reply. The rapping continued.

"Minnie, will you answer the door?"

No answer from the kitchen. The rapping grew more insistent. It was foolish to be frightened, Bess decided; Harry would have laughed at her. The thing to do was to go to the front door and open it. What did she expect? Hamlet's ghost? On 113th Street?

She made herself cross to the door and open it.

The rain. The wind. The Halloween jack o'lantern, grinning at her.

Slowly, she closed the door and turned away. Her heart was pounding, for no reason. No reason at all. No one comes back. After all, she told herself, insanely, his father was a rabbi.

But what about the *dybbuk*?

She started to smile, as Harry would have smiled, you stupid *shiksa*, afraid of things that go bump in the night, it's the thunder, it's the kids in the neighborhood, for Christ's sake it's all done with mirrors, isn't it? Life is done with mirrors.

She walked slowly to the mantel and straightened Mama's picture.

Her sleeve brushed the music box, the music box Harry had given her, and it fell off into a chair, startling her as the lid flew open.

"Rosabelle, sweet Rosabelle . . ."

She picked it up and let it play for a while, cradling it in her hands, like you cradle the face of a child, the child they almost had. Then she placed it on the mantel and closed the lid, gently.

Mama's clock, on the mantel beside it, stopped ticking.

Bess glared up at Mama's picture. Mama smiled. Mama always smiled. Defiantly, Bess opened the face of the old clock, the one that had come all the way from Budapest, and wound the weights and started the pendulum swinging again.

But her hands were shaking.

She started for the stairs and paused, near the kitchen door.

"Minnie? I'm going upstairs to lie down."

This time Minnie heard her.

"Good idea. I'll bring the tea up to you."

Bess started up the steps, and suddenly she shivered. A cold wind was blowing down the stairway, probably an open window upstairs. Probably.

Behind her, the clock stopped ticking again.

She whirled. Mama's picture crashed from the mantel, shattering its glass on the stone of the fireplace, and Bess missed the step and she tumbled down the stairs and she was screaming in fright. . . .

"You're so beautiful when you're scared," he

said, and she screamed again, as the Coney Island roller coaster rushed downward toward the boardwalk a million miles below, the strings of real electric lights glittering in the night, Edison's diamonds, people called them. His right arm was about her waist and she realized his left hand was on her breast, and she screamed once more, the way nice girls always screamed if they were touched where they liked it.

"Stop screaming, I only asked if you wanted to go to bed with me."

"Harry!"

She screamed again. She was supposed to.

"All right, if I have to marry you first, I will."

"Harry, we're going to fall out!"

"Did you hear what I said? I proposed."

"That's the lousiest proposal I ever heard!"

The roller coaster swung into a tight curve, and she felt her body forced against his.

"You got a better offer?" she heard him asking, as she gasped for breath. And his hand moved lower.

"You don't have a penny! You live with your mother! Harry, we're going to get killed!"

They were plunging down again, down and down toward the ocean. She clung to him.

"I don't care," he whispered in her ear, "I don't care as long as we die together."

The roller coaster leveled out for a moment. He could hear her heart pounding.

"Harry? I don't want to die until we make love."

The room was tiny, even for those days, even for the rooms that immigrant families were forced to live in, 69th Street on the East Side, three flights up, freezing in winter, suffocating in summer, but what did you expect? This was the promised land, so you lived on promises, from the landlord, from the bosses, from the Congress. Was it better in the old country?

Harry had tried to brighten it with posters of the great magicians. The table by the brass bedstead was crammed with handcuffs, decks of cards, tricks purchased from the wholesale houses, an oil lamp with a glass shade that would some day be priceless, but right now reeked of kerosene. Home sweet home.

"I want to go home," Bess said. She was sitting up in Harry's bed, her skin glowing pinkly in the lamplight, holding the sheet up to her chin to hide her nakedness. The exhilaration was gone, the madness that had driven them to the tiny apartment, laughing, kissing, touching each other. She had made him go down the hall to the bathroom while she had removed her clothes, and by the time he returned, he was a stranger, a stranger taking off his pants in her presence. The entire nineteenth century was calling to her to remain a virgin. Don't do as I do, do as I say.

"Don't be a hypocrite," Harry said, and started

to unbutton the foolish long underwear. "You're here because you want to be. This isn't a kidnapping."

"How will we live?"

"Don't worry. I'm going to be the greatest magician in the world."

She tried to smile.

"Then change me into a pumpkin."

He laughed.

"Not until midnight."

"Then it'll be too late."

He crossed to the bed. "We're going to have the greatest mindreading act in the history of vaudeville."

"Tonight?"

"No, but soon. Let's practice the code again."

"Do we have to?"

It was a simple code, each word representing the number of a letter in the alphabet. Later, when Harry wrote it out for her, it didn't look difficult:

| | | |
|---------|----|---|
| Pray | 1 | A |
| Answer | 2 | B |
| Say | 3 | C |
| Now | 4 | D |
| Tell | 5 | E |
| Please | 6 | F |
| Speak | 7 | G |
| Quickly | 8 | H |
| Look | 9 | I |
| Be quick | 10 | J |

There are twenty-six letters in the alphabet, and
any of them could be identified by combining the
words—the letter V, for instance, the 22nd letter,
became "Answer answer," 2 and 2. The words had
been carefully selected to sound natural in the
normal dialogue between mindreader and partner.

But nothing seemed normal or natural tonight
to Bess, although she tried her best.

" 'Pray' is A, 'Answer' is B, 'Say' is C, 'Be quick'
is D—"

"No, no, 'Be quick' is J! 'Now' is D."

"Oh, Harry, this is stupid. Why do I have to
learn the code at a time like this?"

"Because you're nervous about what we're going
to do."

"I'm not, I'm not. Harry, put on your robe before you take off your underwear."

"Why?"

"I'm nervous."

He put on the robe. He sighed, but he put on
the robe. He crossed and sat down on the bed,
and took her hand in his, and leaned over and
kissed her. Gently.

"You're so beautiful."

"You sure your mother won't come back home
tonight?"

"She's at my brother Theo's, sitting with the
baby. She comes home in the morning on the
trolley."

He kissed her again, urgently.

"Harry, I changed my mind!"

She sounded frantic now, trying to push him away, to keep his body separated from hers. In those days girls really believed there was a fate worse than death, although no one explained to them that it was made up of a lot of little deaths, as the French called them.

Before she could break loose, Harry had picked up a pair of his handcuffs from the bedtable and snapped them around her wrist.

"Harry!"

"You might as well learn the whole act. I don't wanna have to chase you around the room."

He snapped the other handcuff about his own wrist. Now they were chained together. There was no escape. His arms were about her, his body pressed hers, and she knew they were all lies, the stories her mother had told her, and she wanted the little deaths, she wanted him, and as they kissed again she whispered, "Please . . . be quick. And I'm not using the code."

He had the sheet off her in an instant, her naked body unashamed in the lamplight, his naked body covering hers.

His mother's voice called, "Ehrich? Ehrincha? You're home already?"

"Jesus Christ!" It was Bess. She had never used those words before except in prayer. She tried to leap out of one side of the bed as Harry leaped out of the other and their handcuffed hands yanked

them back on the bed together as the door opened
and Mrs. Weiss entered carrying a paper bag.

"From Theo I brought you some chicken soup—"
She never finished.

"Mama," said Harry, "I'd like you to meet my
wife."

# ACT TWO

~~~~~~~~~~~

CECILA STEINER WEISS was an unusual woman,
a woman out of her time, a woman insisting on her
own identity in a century dedicated to keeping
women in their place. George Sand demonstrated
her individuality by wearing pants; Cecilia Weiss
didn't have to. She was the head of the family and
always had been.

In Budapest she had insisted on marrying a man
twenty-five years her senior, for the foolish reason
that she was in love with him. Her family protested that he was a rabbi, a bad rabbi at that,
barely making a living. But Cecilia knew he was
a man of sensitivity and pride and courage, and
that she could make him into the kind of husband
she wanted. It was not easy to be Jewish in Hun-
gary in those days; for that matter, it's no picnic

today. And all of Cecilia's plans for the future of
the family they had started were blasted to bits
because Maier Samuel Weiss insisted on holding
his head up high. A proud man. A small, proud
Jew in the era of the pogrom.

"Your father killed a man, I never told you."
That was the way Cecilia finally explained to
Harry, long afterward, why they had come to
America.

"In Budapest, an important man, believe me, he
called your father a name, such a name, a dirty
Jew bastard, someone else might not hear, but your
father heard. He challenged him to a duel, such a
thing had never happened before, every Jew in
Budapest would have had to fight a duel.

"The man laughed, it would be something he
should tell his friends, he had shot a rabbi in the
*kishke*, but he didn't know your father. Papa never
held such a thing, a pistol, before, he was scared,
but he killed him, God gave him the strength, he
killed him, not for himself, for all of us, for you,
for me, for everybody. So we had to leave, our
little family, we had to leave our home, our Budapest, everything we had, it was a miracle we got
out, such a thing could not be allowed, a Jew
winning a duel, next thing they would want to live
on the same street with Gentiles."

Because they had friends there, the family came
to Appleton, Wisconsin. It was hardly a shrewd
move. Of all the places in the world that didn't

need a Talmudic scholar who spoke only Hungarian, Yiddish, and Hebrew, Appleton was close to the top of the list.

They arrived in 1876, the year the nation celebrated its Centennial and baseball founded the National League, the year Custer had his last stand and Samuel Langhorne Clemens published *The Adventures of Tom Sawyer*. The year Alexander Graham Bell patented the telephone. He should have taken a moment to pick it up and call Maier Samuel Weiss and warn him. Soon there were five hungry boys and one hungry girl in his family, making them the majority of the local Jewish community.

As the years went by, Cecilia was the one who brought order out of chaos. While Maier studied the Talmud, everyone else was put to work in this strange country that had no respect for Hungarian philosophers. Ehrich got two jobs at once, delivering newspapers and shining shoes, and became the primary breadwinner. On his bar mitzvah, his father took him aside and made him promise that, now that he was thirteen and a man, Ehrich would always take care of his mother. Since that was what Ehrich was already doing, and since he thought that was his father's job, he decided that night to fulfill the American dream: he ran away from home.

Mama was heartbroken, although Ehrich wrote often and sent back a little money when he got a job with a circus. Cecilia decided that her husband

would never succeed in converting the state of
Wisconsin to Judaism; where he should go was the
Budapest of America, New York City, where at
least there were more synagogues than cows. The
courageous rabbi faced up to the challenge and, at
the age of sixty-four, alone, he set out to make a
living as a Hebrew scholar in a Jewish community
that already had enough Hebrew scholars to teach
a whole generation to read from right to left.

Ehrich, on the road somewhere in Texas, heard
about it, and he was frightened by the thought of
his father facing up to the tide of immigration
that was pouring past the Statue of Liberty to find
refuge and a living on the East Side of Manhattan.
The immigrants were jammed into tiny rooms,
exploited, cheated, hated, crowded into sweat-
shops, deprived of everything except hope. Years
later they would emerge, singing, to become the
heart and life and muscle of a great nation, and
eventually attempt to close the doors against anyone else who wanted to be as lucky as they had
been. But for the moment New York was a jungle,
and Ehrich knew his prideful father was likely to
challenge the whole city to a duel.

So Ehrich Weiss, at fourteen, made his way to
New York, and he and Papa had a reunion in a
restaurant on the East Side over a plate of goulash,
the proud old man and his *meshugeneh* son, who
had been earning a living hanging upside down
by his heels and picking up needles with his eye-

lashes. Ehrich got a job in a tie factory, cutting linings, and eventually they sent for Cecilia and the whole brood from Appleton, Wisconsin, and moved into a tiny apartment.

Cecilia found New York more to her liking than the Middle West. Soon she was like the other immigrant mothers, worrying, clucking, shielding her children from tuberculosis by having them drink seltzer water, "two cents plain." It probably didn't do any good, but neither did the doctors. Everyone worked, everyone went to school except Ehrich, who was learning to open handcuffs and running the hundred-yard dash for the Pastime Athletic Club, developing those startling muscles, and had no time for education; he'd already gotten his Ph.D. from the circus. There were five brothers, Ehrich and Theo and Nathan and Leo and Joseph, and a sister, and everyone had a good job but Papa, which meant life was normal.

Rabbi Maier Weiss, pretending to be serene, pretending to be content here in this country where he understood no one and no one understood him, could not pretend to his God. God understood. He took Maier, quietly, to a happier place.

Cecilia cried for a week. This gentle man, this gentle proud man, had been her companion and her lover and her inspiration; he had also been her bed of nails, her frustration, and somewhat of a *shlemiehl*, but she had loved him. How could he leave her? she cried out. How could he leave her

alone with all his normal children and Ehrich the
*meshugeneh*?

She went to work herself to fill the gap, bringing
home piecework to sew on her Singer in the living
room while, one by one, the children struck out
on their own or went off to get an education. All
but Ehrich, who got his brother Theo to join him
in a magic act called the Houdini Brothers. Ehrich
adopted the name from that of Robert-Houdin, the
great French magician, whose country had once
sent him to settle a revolt in Algeria by demon-
strating to the Arab chieftains that his magic was
more potent than that of the fanatic Marabouts,
who had been advising the chiefs to fight against
France. Robert-Houdin put on a show of magic
the likes of which had not been heard of since the
the days of Scheherazade, and the revolt was ended.
The story fascinated Ehrich and he adapted the
name to Houdini, and later wrote a book about
his idol. Later on in life Robert-Houdin's widow
refused to see Harry Houdini, and Harry wrote a
book *against* him.

Ehrich and Theo were doing their act at Coney
Island when Ehrich met Beatrice Raymond, who
had also changed her name, from Wilhelmina
Rahner, when she became one of the Floral Sisters,
"neat song and dance artistes."

It was a whirlwind ten-day romance, winding up
in Ehrich's bed; but at the final moment, the only
climax had been a shriek from Mama.

Now Cecilia Weiss waited, in her living room, pretending to be busy sewing some piecework from the factory.

After delaying as long as he could, in part to find the key to the handcuffs but mainly to calm Bess down, Ehrich finally came out of the bedroom, pulling up his suspenders and tying his tie, determined not to give Mama the satisfaction of seeing him upset.

He crossed to her and waited. She kept sewing, not deigning to look around. Finally, he leaned down and kissed her on the neck. She kept on sewing, her feet working the treadle, her hands moving the material past the busy needle.

"I'm sorry," he said. "I should have told you about her, but everything happened very fast."

"I noticed." She bit off a thread that didn't need to be bitten off.

"She does an act with her sisters, she sings."

"Sings, too?"

Harry caught the irony. He walked around the sewing machine and put his hand on the wheel to stop it.

"Mama, she's a wonderful girl."

Cecilia brushed his hand aside and resumed her work.

"So what temple did you get married in without telling me?"

The accent was unmistakably Yiddish. Cecilia

was an educated woman, but English was not her
tongue; the rhythms of the expressive language of
her youth could not be broken, no matter how
hard she tried. Perhaps she didn't really want to
break them. It is one of the few truly international
languages, more than a language, a bond, a token
of common sorrows, common burdens, a language
of expressive alliteration and onomatopoeic sounds
known only to the initiated, who by the very token
of their knowledge of it must be your friend. And
the fear she was concealing had been concealed
by Jewish mothers in similar circumstances since
before the Diaspora.

"So what temple did you get married in without
telling me?"

"No temple. City Hall."

"City Hall! You think God has ever been to
City Hall?"

"Not lately."

"A wedding ring I didn't see."

"I didn't have enough for the ring. We borrowed
one."

"Tell the truth, she's a *shiksa*?"

Finally, it was out, the word, the fear, she
couldn't look her son in the eye, she knew the
answer. Bess had entered from the bedroom in
time to hear. She may not have understood the
word, but there was no mistaking the tone. She
was dressed now, and frightened, but she was Bess,
and she would hide no longer.

"I'm a Catholic, Mrs. Weiss," she said, much too loudly.

Cecilia turned and stared at her.

"The worst kind," she said finally.

"Mama, shut up!" Ehrich had become Harry now, Harry who was a married man, a *mensch*. He had brought his bride home and would protect her, even against the mother he had grown to love to such a degree his brothers joked about it. He would continually bring Mama gifts, give her half his earnings, partly to expiate the guilt he felt for having run away after having promised Papa, at his bar mitzvah, to watch over her. That first night in New York when he met Papa, they had gone back to the rabbi's meager room and Maier Weiss, proud Maier Weiss, had taken off his belt and given his young son a *schlag* so he wouldn't ever forget, so he wouldn't ever break his word again.

"Papa, stop! If it's such a terrible thing," Ehrich had howled, "*God* will punish me."

"Maybe He doesn't have a belt," Rabbi Weiss had said reasonably, and hit his son again.

But it was more than guilt, it was a filial love that would be suspect in this age of Freudian interpretation of anything so unnatural as innocence. The truth is that after Cecilia Weiss died, Harry Houdini had every one of the letters she had written to him in her lifetime translated into English—Mama wrote in German or Yiddish—and kept them with him so he could read and reread them daily; and when he was buried, the letters were buried beside him in the coffin, the coffin he had used in his act.

But now, at this moment, her son standing before her defiantly, the Catholic he had brought into her home equally defiant, Cecilia knew in her heart there was no way to turn the clock back. It was done, for all time. Life would never be as it had been. Never could she forgive Ehrich for what he had done, much as she loved him. He hadn't done it only to her. He had done it to all of them, who had fought so hard, who had struggled for so long to preserve—what? The pride of being different? Or something more?

She didn't speak for a while. She turned away from the sewing machine, picked up a needle, and pretended to thread it, her mind a long distance away, thousands of miles, the park in Budapest, a little rabbi with trembling hands looking into the barrel of a dueling pistol and facing death because he had to face it, for reasons his son obviously never understood.

Finally, because she had to say something, she said to Bess, "Your family has money?"

"Well, no. My mother's a widow."

"So you're going to live in your mother's house?"

"No, Mrs. Weiss. She locked me out."

Mrs. Weiss looked at her quizzically, the meaning not clear.

"You did something to her?"

"Yes," Bess said. "I fell in love with your son."

Mrs. Weiss dropped the needle and thread. She knew she faced a battle. She retrieved the little spool and found another needle as she turned to her son again.

"Ehrich, why must you always give problems? A nice Orthodox girl with a *tuchas* you couldn't marry? In nine months, a baby, a boy, believe me. This skinny *shiksa*?" She stared at Bess. "If it happens at all, it'll be by Caesarian, how will you afford?" She held out her hand. "Help me thread this needle."

Harry took the needle and the thread from her.

"Don't worry, Mama. Bess is going to take Theo's place in the act with me, she's a great singer, some day we'll play Hammerstein's Victoria, top of the bill, biggest attraction in America!"

And he stuffed the needle and thread into his mouth. With a shriek, Mama leaped to her feet.

"Ehrich! You'll kill yourself!"

She reached for the thread and started to pull it out, and with it came thirty more needles, all carefully strung on the white thread.

"My son, the *meshugeneh* magacian," Cecilia murmured, hearing Bess's laughter.

"Your son, the Great Houdini!" Harry insisted.

"Some Great Houdini. You think I could write the relatives in Budapest, Ehrich spends all his time opening handcuffs? Day and night, practice, practice, with his toes he unties knots, what for?

Your brother Leo is going to be a doctor, your brother Nathan is going to be a lawyer, but you—"

"My brother the doctor borrowed two bucks from me last week."

"He has to buy books, for college."

"Books he has, he wanted to go to a cat house."

"At least he won't marry one of the cats!"

Bess gasped. Harry slapped his mother, the first time, the last time, but he slapped her, and the sky had fallen, she turned her back on him, but not far enough so he couldn't see how she was suffering.

"I'm sorry, Mama, I'm sorry!"

"A *shiksa*!" Cecilia wailed, the wail of a hundred generations against the wailing wall of their sons' sexuality. "A *shiksa*! Your poor father is turning over in his grave!"

Bess touched Harry's sleeve.

"Harry, let's get out of here," she said, hurt, embarrassed, humiliated, wanting to run, to run anyplace.

"Where will you go?" Mama asked, her attitude changing instantly when there was a chance this girl might take her son away. "Sit down!"

"But you just said—"

"Sit down, sit down, who do you think I am, your mother? Ehrich, give her a chair."

"Mama—"

"Shhh, Ehrich, you sit down, too, or maybe you want you should hit me again?"

"I told you I'm sorry!"

"You shouldn't be, what I said was terrible, on top of it I called her a *shiksa*."

Harry had pulled out a chair for Bess, who sat, slowly, as Mrs. Weiss sat down opposite her, across the table with the bowl of wax fruit in the middle, surrounded by the piecework from the factory that had to be finished, somehow, that night.

Mrs. Weiss sighed. She looked at her daughter-in-law carefully. The girl was pretty, in a Gentile way. Her face was flushed with anger. On her it looked good, Cecilia thought, and she had spirit, she was a fighter, which the old lady secretly admired. This was a proud girl. Pride was one thing this family understood, from experience, from bitter experience.

To Bess, she repeated, "I called you a *shiksa*, you can call me a *yenta*."

"What does that mean?"

Mrs. Weiss shrugged.

"Look at me, that's what it means."

"Mama," Harry said, but she stopped him.

"Please. This is between me and the *goya*." She turned back to Bess. "How could I expect you should understand how I feel?" She searched for a way to begin. "Mrs. Weiss—" she stopped, halted by the incongruity, throwing a look at her son. "*Mrs. Weiss!*"

She reached out her hand, to touch Bess's.

"Look good at me. I'm five thousand years old."

Harry's mother frightened Bess. She didn't understand her, the accent was strange, the words stranger. But looking into her eyes, the five thousand years became comprehensible.

"From the time of Abraham," Cecilia continued. "You think that's nothing, five thousand years, the same people? Who else can say it? Do I have to tell you what it cost us? With fire they tried to finish us, with swords, with guns, with hate . . ." She paused, to be certain her daughter-in-law took notice. "You think I want to see them do it with love?"

And finally, Bess knew. This was what it was all about. The desperate struggle not to disappear. The cry of a race.

"I understand." It was almost the truth.

"Some of my best friends have been Catholics," Cecilia told her. "One of them for almost a month."

Harry had crossed and put his arms around his mother.

"I can't fight any more," Mama said. "Young people, what does it mean to them? You can have my room, the bed doesn't squeak. That I couldn't stand, somebody making half a Gentile in my house."

"It's going to be all right, Mama. We'll have a family without prejudice. From now on."

Mrs. Weiss smiled at her son. As long as he was still hers, the battle was going well.

"Absolutely," she said. "You'll get married again

in a temple by a rabbi, and the girl will convert."

So it was settled. Until Bess got to her feet.

"I'm a Catholic, Mrs. Weiss. I'm going to remain a Catholic."

Cecilia whirled on her, the mask falling now, the hurt and the anger making her voice tremble.

"Then get out!" She pointed to the door. She meant it.

Bess stood firm. Harry crossed to her. The first family struggle was the most important, he knew. This was the bridge that had to be crossed; Bess had to understand how much it meant.

"It's only a ceremony," he told her. "A religious ceremony, it takes only a few minutes, but to my mother it's important."

"Oh, I want the ceremony, Harry, I want it for your sake."

He breathed a sigh. What a wonderful girl.

"But we'll have a wedding in the Catholic church first."

From the way she said it, they all knew there was no turning back. The lines were drawn. Mrs. Weiss waited. Harry didn't rush to her side. She turned on him, tears of anger in her eyes. How could she have failed, how could they all have failed with this one *meshugeneh* son?

"You do this to your dead father," she told him. "Till the day I die I won't forgive you."

It was to be the cross Ehrich would bear for

the rest of his life. No, not the cross. The Mogen David.

Mrs. Rahner showed up for the Catholic ceremony, but she left immediately afterward, a tight-lipped German woman who felt disgraced, as did Cecilia Weiss, but who had no forgiveness in her. She had eight other daughters and a son. She had to hurry back home to protect them from themselves.

Harry and Bess went through the Orthodox ceremony with the rabbi for the benefit of Mrs. Weiss and Harry's brothers and sister, and he took his bride home to live with his mother, but beyond that they both knew there was no real forgiveness here, either. And probably there never would be.

The Great Houdinis broke in their act together in Coney Island, on the street of cabarets called the Bowery, where such notables as Irving Berlin, Eddie Cantor, and Jimmy Durante later got their start. They struggled to convince their rowdy audiences that sleight-of-hand and miraculous escapes and a few gentle songs made a better evening's entertainment than throwing a pitcher of beer at your neighbor or visiting the red-light district around the corner. 1896 will be remembered as the year ragtime was born and the Great Houdinis almost died.

They left the big city, possibly by request, and

began the wandering life of the itinerant entertainer that marked the beginning of vaudeville. They traveled back and forth across the country playing one-night stands, living from hand to mouth. The truth is, the act wasn't very good. Harry was too short to fit the popular image of the tall, dignified, frock-coated magician; and Bess didn't have enough curves to do justice to the tights she wore, with considerable embarrassment, at Harry's insistence. Mrs. Weiss had been right: she didn't have much of a *tuchas*, and *tucha*s was what was selling then, as now.

The early years passed, as they struggled to survive. Chicago and San Francisco were followed by St. Joe, Missouri, where they had their interlude in the graveyard, because seances had become fashionable. In 1898 at 9:40 in the evening of a warm Cuban spring, 250 American sailors had been blown up aboard the U.S. battleship *Maine* in Havana harbor, and the Spanish-American War was in full swing, fanned by the patriotic ardor of the Hearst press. One of the unavoidable products of any war is the wholesale death of young men, and the sense of mortality that comes to the living makes them seek some assurance that what we have here, on this unworkable planet, is not the whole ball game. Most religions gain their popularity by assuring the faithful that life is only the trailer; the feature comes on later for those who have paid their dues to the Church.

What church that happens to be seems unimportant. But there are many who are unwilling to wait, who want some assurance now that there is a future worth sacrificing the present for. And there are many who can't accept that their young men are gone forever. After every war, there is always a willing audience for those who claim to be in contact with the eternal mystery.

In the last century, the spiritualist movement started when Katie and Margaret Fox, two young girls in Hydeville, New York, frightened their superstitious mother by bouncing an apple on a string over the floor at night. They could even produce strange rappings when they were tied hand and foot. No one realized these two innocents could snap their big toes against the second toe and produce the noise. Others followed, among them the miraculous Ira Erastus and William Henry Davenport, who could be tied within a cabinet while a tambourine danced across the floor nearby, and Daniel Dunglas Home, to whom the spirits spoke through a prearranged code, rapping once for yes, twice for no. No one ever thought it strange that there was no code for maybe.

Belief in the other world grew to astonishing proportions; the most learned men, the most prominent writers, politicians, governors and presidents believed, or professed to believe. Apparently, there were votes beyond the grave. The Spanish-American War brought it all to a climax, and it didn't take

the realistic and materialistic Harry Houdini long
to realize there was a living in the dead. So he
and the unwilling Bess turned to this new field of
communication; there were sources of information
in every small town, city clerks or church sextons
who had the susceptible citizens tabbed and would
give you a list of their names, and statistics on
their most beloved past relatives, for a modest price.
They even advertised in show-business periodicals,
which no one west of Tenth Avenue ever read, so
there was no danger, if you confined your playing
time to the Bible Belt.

Some Fundamentalists, of course, might have
been a little puzzled if they had known the voice
of their departed aunt was speaking to them through
the son of a rabbi; but the Lord moves in mysterious ways His wonders to perform. Eventually,
Harry became frightened, or conscience-stricken,
and, urged by Bess, gave up robbing churchyards
of information. The act returned to its original
form; Harry felt purged, but still hungry.

He wangled them a job in the Welsh Brothers
Circus, sharing half a freight car with the trained
seals, who were eating a lot better than they were.
When that folded, Harry got a booking with a
traveling tent show. Their salary was twenty dollars
a week for the two of them, and they also had to
appear in the opening olio, "Ten Nights in a Bar-
room." Bess also had to sing several solos, and
Harry occasionally doubled for the Wild Man of

Borneo, especially on payday when their envelope was late. They didn't seem to be making much progress, and what married life they had was sandwiched in between costume changes.

There was an argument one night, the sort of inevitable domestic squabble that all young couples go through and survive if there is enough mutual understanding, and Harry reluctantly agreed that if they didn't make it to the top of the bill soon, to save their marriage they would give up showbiz, if that's what they were in.

East Hartford, Connecticut, was to be the final test. If you couldn't make it in East Hartford, you couldn't make it anyplace.

An audience of hard-bitten farmers and their wives, and a few businessmen starting an insurance business, were in the tent that night to watch the Great Houdinis perform their Metamorphosis, the Greatest Novelty Mystery Act in the World. Or so the handbills proclaimed. The bills even contained a complete description of how it would be performed: "All the Apparatus used in this Act is inspected by a Committee selected from the Audience. Mons. Houdini's hands are fastened with manacles, he is securely tied in a bag and the knots are sealed, then placed in a massive trunk which is locked and strapped, the trunk is then rolled into a small cabinet, and Mlle. Houdini"—note that apparently, despite her lack of *tuchas,* it had been decided that Bess could add sex to the per-

formance if she and Harry appeared to be having
a liaison rather than a marriage. They were French,
weren't they?—"Mlle. Houdini draws the curtain
and claps her hand three times, at the last clap
of her hands the curtain is drawn open by Mons.
Houdini and Mlle. Houdini has disappeared, and
upon the trunk being opened, she is found in his
place in the bag, the seals unbroken and her hands
manacled in precisely the same manner as were
Mons. Houdini's when first entering the bag." And
then, in italics, the handbill concluded: "Just think
over this, the time consumed in making the change
is THREE SECONDS!"

Harry should have added, "If we're lucky."

This night, they had decided to add one of Bess's
songs to the repertoire. As the handcuffs were
fastened about his wrists, Harry and Bess sang the
sentimental melody of a song hit of the day:

> *"Rosabelle, sweet Rosabelle,*
> *I love you more than I can tell.*
> *O'er me you cast a spell . . .*
> *I love you,*
> *My Rosabelle!"*

The silken bag was pulled over his head and
impressively tied and sealed, and he lay down
within the trunk as Bess closed the lid and locked
it, placing the key down her bosom, then allowed

the Committee to tie the trunk firmly with rope
and check the lock.

She stepped forward to the drape.

"I close the curtain like this!" she cried dramatically, closing the curtains with a sweep of her hand
and disappearing from view behind them. The audience heard her clap her hands together three times
and then the curtain was swept aside by a trium-
phant Harry, resplendent in his tuxedo, out of the
handcuffs, out of the trunk, which was still sealed,
locked, and roped; and Bess had disappeared.

"And here is the Great Houdini!" Harry shouted,
to an amazed audience of two or three who hadn't
seen the trick performed before.

Wise guys, he thought. Wise apple knockers.
Wait till they see the rest of it! He milked them
for a bow, then turned grandly to the trunk and
sang:

> *"Rosabelle, sweet Rosabelle,*
> *Come on out, dear Rosabelle . . .!"*

With a dramatic gesture, he untied the ropes and
threw them free of the trunk. From within it came
Bess's pure soprano, "O'er me you cast a spell!"

And, for the finale, Harry sang, "Come on out,
my Rosabelle!" and slapped the trunk three times.
The lid was to fly open to reveal Bess, in the silken
bag, wearing the handcuffs. But it didn't. The

trunk remained securely locked.

Perspiring somewhat, Harry rapped on the trunk again. He heard Bess's voice, from somewhere within its depths: "Harry, I can't get out of this goddam thing."

Harry smiled for the audience and motioned to the orchestra—one drum and a tinny piano—to play louder. He whispered to Bess, as loudly as he dared.

"Press the gimmick! Press the gimmick! It'll release the lock!"

"I can't find the stupid gimmick." Bess's voice was showing signs of panic. "It's dark in here, I'm suffocating, I'm gonna faint!"

"Rosabelle," sang Harry, "sweet Rosabelle, come on out, dear Rosabelle!"

He kicked the trunk desperately.

"Harry," came the feeble voice from within, "break the lock and let me out!"

"I can't! That would finish the act! Come out the back way, the way you got in."

"It's stuck."

"Use the key."

"I dropped it down my breast and now I can't find it."

"Rosabelle," sang Harry, "Sweet Rosabelle, come on out, dear Rosabelle!"

The audience was hooting now, clapping derisively, getting to their feet, everyone leaving to see the two-headed calf in the next tent.

The manager was in the wings, gesturing to Harry to get the act off the stage.

Desperately, he tried again:

> *"O'er me you cast a spell,*
> *Come on out, dear Rosabelle!"*

"Harry," came the voice, "break the goddam lock, I think I'm gonna throw up!"

The urgency could not be denied. Harry dashed offstage, grabbed a fire axe, leaped back, smashed the lock, and threw back the trunk lid. Like the trouper she was, Bess sprang to her feet, disheveled, perspiring, nauseous, but smiling her biggest smile at the audience, or what was left of it.

"*Presto!*" shouted Harry Houdini.

The curtain rolled down with a merciful thud.


There is nothing lonelier than the sound of a train whistle in the night, the banshee wail of steam escaping into nothingness. It echoed into the consciousness of Harry and Bess, seated forlornly in an empty coach of the New York, New Haven and Hartford's Midnight Special, their meager luggage on the seat opposite them, the remains of their sparse supper on a napkin on Bess's lap as she munched an apple.

Finally, Harry spoke.

"I told the manager we were gonna quit his lousy show anyway," he grumbled. "The bastard didn't have to yell."

"You don't know how relieved I am. Aren't you?"

Harry didn't answer. His silence shouted at her.

"Harry, you haven't changed your mind, have you? You promised me!"

She bit into the apple fiercely, venting her anger on its juicy innocence.

"You know how much money we have left?" she asked. "Five dollars! Five dollars to last the rest of our lives!"

Finally, Harry spoke.

"Ten," he said, as if it were millions.

"You forget, you always make me send half of everything we make to your mother. I'm saving her the core."

She held up what was left of the apple.

"Don't you ever talk about Mama like that!"

It was one subject, Bess knew, that upset him. That's why she continually brought it up. At least, it made him speak to her.

"Harry, are we going home or aren't we? I don't want to spend one more night in some fleabag boarding house, fighting off the cockroaches and the overaged leading men. Or stealing names from a graveyard so you can bring back the dead at a matinee."

The conductor entered, a large Irish individual, anxious to get back to the rear platform and enjoy the flask of Jack Daniels in his jacket pocket. It was a cold December night, a man needed protection against frostbite and the sad realization that he was an exploited member of the laboring class, when by instinct and inclination he would have made a fine, bloated capitalist. It was the age of the I.W.W. and Emma Goldman, the governor of Idaho had been blown to bits just the week before by a bomb planted by striking miners. It was a grand, bloody fight to be in on either side, although the conductor instinctively knew that rich was better. "Tickets, please, tickets." The familiar litany was somewhat comforting to him. He took them from Harry's hand and glanced at them.

"We'll be in Bridgeport in an hour," he said, mechanically punching holes in them. Punch, brothers, punch with care, went the doggerel of the time, punch in the presence of the passenjare.

"Bridgeport?" Bess was startled. "We're going through to New York!"

The conductor glanced at the tickets again briefly. He never made mistakes.

"Not with these," he said, and stuffed them into the top of the seat behind them, and headed for the rear platform and his dreams.

Harry felt Bess's look. He shifted, uncomfortably, on the plush seat.

"I got us a booking," he said defiantly.

"You promised!"

"Sure, I promised. I didn't know I could get a booking."

There is nothing so infuriating to a woman as honesty. From a man.

"Harry, your mother wrote there's a good job for you in the tie factory!"

"What's a good job in a tie factory?"

"You can't do this! We agreed! I've been counting on it! I've been dreaming of it! You'd get a regular job, we'd have our own room, the same room every night, but you've been lying all the time, you never for a minute intended—"

He tried to put his arms around her.

"Bess, listen, I can't help it. I'm a magician. That's what I am. That's all I am."

No, he was more than that. Should she tell him now? She decided against it.

"For God's sake," she said, "what's so important about being a magician?"

And she pushed him away.

How do you explain your life in five minutes on the New York, New Haven and Hartford?

"All right, Mrs. Catholic," he said, and moved away from her. He had to make the attempt.

"You ever work in a tie factory with two dozen stinking old men, where you never see the sun all day?"

He could see it, the sewing machines, row after row, the bales of material, the guttering gas lights, the experience shared by a million men and a million women over a decade, to whom America was needle and thread and backache and eight cents an hour. Could he make her see it, too, his *goyishe* wife?

"You ever see your father spit on because he was an immigrant and a Jew?"

He was on his feet now, his back turned to her, ashamed to expose himself this way, but she had to know. She had a right. Whether she wanted to or not.

"A wise man, a proud man, but he took it because he had to try to feed us. I saw it kill him." He turned to her now. She saw the look. This wasn't Ehrich Weiss, this was Houdini; the look, the stare, was to become famous, it was what set him apart from ordinary men, the eyes that were looking at you and through you to something beyond ordinary experience. Possibly next week's check.

But he was deadly serious now.

"I'm going to fight," he said, and she knew he could never be Maier Samuel Weiss, who held a pistol only once. Every day of Harry's life was to be a duel.

Now he was sitting beside her, taking her hand, as if the touch would help communicate what he felt.

"You know what a magician does?"

He knew she didn't really know. "He escapes. From Hester Street, from Rivington Street, from the noise and the smell and the horse manure, he escapes. Colored lights, fancy costumes, making miracles, it's the second best thing to being God."

He turned away from her, embarrassed that he had shown so much of himself to his own wife. He didn't know if she had understood a word.

He felt her hand on his shoulder.

"Harry," she said to him, softly, "you know you'll never settle for second best."

He started to laugh, the tension over. The laughter poured out; she had understood, she probably had understood before he said it.

He should have told her he loved her.

Instead he said, "Better watch out, you're gonna give *shiksas* a good name."

She kissed him, but he broke away and took out his handkerchief.

"Come on, if we're gonna escape, we gotta practice."

He tied the handkerchief over his eyes.

"Not again," she protested wearily. "It's one o'clock in the morning!"

"Ladies and gentlemen, watch closely. Through my mysterious powers of telepathy, I shall guess whatever the little lady has in her hand."

He motioned to Bess. She hesitated a moment,

then she said, *"Pray tell* me, sir . . ."

"P," said Harry promptly.

"Pray speak . . ."

"R . . ."

"Tell . . ."

"E . . ."

"Speak . . ."

"G . . ."

Bess paused, waiting.

"Is that all," Harry asked, puzzled, "P,r,e,g—?"

He stopped short. She had taken his hand and placed it against her abdomen.

"Jesus Christ!" he shouted. "Pregnant!"

"It's the second best thing to being God, Harry."


P. T. Barnum had shown the way. There's one born every minute, and two to take him. Bread and circuses. Lions 12, Christians 0, and the mob forgot they were being taxed to pay the Roman politicians double the cost of the Colosseum. It wasn't skill that paid off, Harry had discovered, it was showmanship. He knew every gimmick of the magician's trade, he could do wonders with a pack of cards, he could escape from most restraints with the power of his body and the knowledge of his mind, and he was still a failure.

Now, here in Bridgeport, came the inspiration that was to shape his career. It had been coming to him, bit by bit, over the past year or so. Martin

Beck, the entrepreneur, had told him to forget the magic in his act and concentrate on the escapes, and Beck had been right. The human race is trying to escape; it would like to believe freedom is something man can eventually achieve. Harry had already escaped from the San Francisco jail before an audience of reporters. But that wasn't enough. It only showed up in the printed word and the photograph, after it was over. The act itself must be viewed by thousands. They all wanted to see him die, why not give them a chance?

Harry visited the newspaper offices and used his last resources to buy drinks for the reporters. He found freedom of the press much freer after a double Scotch.

It appeared on the second page of the newspaper the next morning, exactly as he had laid it out:

**THE BRIDGEPORT JOURNAL**
**CHALLENGES**
**HOUDINI**
**to DIVE into the FREEZING ATLANTIC OCEAN**
**MANACLED by MEMBERS**
**of the**
**POLICE FORCE**
**SUNDAY, DEC. 10TH, 12 NOON SHARP**
**BRIDGEPORT PIER**

Even Harry was startled by the size of the turn-
out. They crowded the pier, men, women, and
children, hanging over the railing, turning up their
collars against the blustering wind, hoping against
hope they would be lucky enough to see a stranger
kill himself in the dive, or at least freeze to death.
After all, some of them had skipped church. They
deserved a good show.

Two burly sergeants of the Bridgeport police
fastened the shiny manacles about his wrists. These
were massive, old-fashioned restraints which had
held a hundred prisoners before him. Harry, of
course, had managed to study them carefully the
day before. He never left anything like that to
chance. He had been down to the police station,
engaging the officers in jovial conversation, standing them to a growler of beer with his last dime,
while Bess, innocent Bess, had managed the rest.
Who would have imagined her concealing a bit of
soft wax in her skirt and sitting on the bunch of
keys as they lay on the desk? Harry's quick eye
had selected the right impression and a locksmith
had quietly done the rest. Bess's *tuchas* was small,
but talented.

Now Harry was confident, hands raised above
his head in the shining handcuffs in a gesture to
the crowd. Several photographers maneuvered their
heavy cameras into position to get a shot. The
friendly reporters were making notes. The wind

was biting, but Harry, dressed only in a bathing suit, scarcely noticed. This was his big moment. Here was the attention he had longed for. All he had to do was follow through. A thorough body search had revealed his key, and it had been tossed into the ocean. But so what—Bess had another one.

He took her arm as the police escorted him through the throng to the railing. They spoke in whispers.

"It's freezing," she murmured. "You'll drown."

"That's what they all hope. That's why they're here."

"I don't want you to do this for me."

"Not only you," Harry told her. "We're going to have another mouth to feed."

"You mean, beside your mother's?"

Before he could answer she put her arms about his neck and kissed him, passionately, turning her head so the others could not see the metal as it passed from her lips to his. Then it was done, and she moved away, fear turning her colder than the wind.

Harry climbed up on the railing and posed for the photographers again as the crowd pushed closer, climbed to the roof of the buildings, growing impatient. What right had he to continue breathing? It was almost time for lunch.

"Get the name right, boys," Harry shouted to the reporters. "Harry Houdini! At the Granada

Theatre all this week."

One of the reporters called out to the police, "Hey, Kelly, you sure those are real cuffs?"

"Same ones we had on your father last time he beat up your mother!"

There was laughter at that, partly because it was true.

"He'll never get 'em off!" shouted Kelly proudly.

"Damn right," the other sergeant whispered to him. "I jammed birdshot in the keyholes. Hope that New York kike knows how to swim."

He grinned at his companion.

Bess, standing just behind them, had overheard. Only a hacksaw would get the handcuffs off now. She pushed her way through, her face white, shouting, screaming, "Harry! Harry, STOP!"

But he was already leaping from the railing, arching gracefully toward the ocean, handcuffed hands extended before him, the useless key clenched between his teeth so as not to be jarred loose by the impact. The crowd leaned over farther, some shouting, some holding their breath, some even hoping he might live through it so they could get to see him kill himself another day.

And then there was the splash, and he disappeared beneath the water. And he didn't reappear.

There was a sudden silence. It had been a game. Death had seemed only a headline. Now it was there, staring them in the face. Some realized it was always staring them in the face, and turned away.

Bess clutched at the railing. She knew what was happening. Harry, under the water, was attempting to fit the key into the keyhole. He had discovered by now he had been tricked. He was trying, somehow, someway, to slip the handcuffs off his wrists, and failing, and feeling the oxygen slipping away from him, the strangulation in the back of his throat as he refused to give up, he refused to admit failure before the largest audience of his life, to hear their laughter, the laughter that could mean the end of his career, what career there had been.

Finally, with his last gasp, he broke the surface, the hands still firmly fastened in steel, unable to use them to swim, his only hope to remain alive. The icy water numbed his body, his muscles refused to function, he floundered desperately and went under, water in his lungs so cold it froze his insides, and still he struggled. Not in Bridgeport, he kept telling himself, what a lousy place to drown, Bess, I'm sorry. Let me live, let me live, *baruch atah Adenoi*, the prayers of his father ran through his brain, God help me, God help me, and if there is no God how about a good swimmer?

A rowboat had been standing by for just such an emergency, and now one of the rowers threw off his slicker and dove into the water. He reached Harry's side, but the cold numbed him, too. His fingers couldn't grasp the body; Harry slipped beneath the waves, the Good Samaritan following.

Somehow, he got an arm hooked through Harry's manacled hands, fought his way to the surface, and the boat was there, another rower moving it into position, and above them, the crowd, cheated of the final spectacle they had anticipated, raced down the pier toward where the two had surfaced, shouting and cheering and hoping to witness at least a good case of pneumonia.

Bess, left alone, was clutching at the railing again, and then clutching at her abdomen, and collapsing, unseen and unnoticed, to the snow-swept planking of the deserted pier.

The crowd didn't know it, but inside her what they had come to see had happened.

But it was such a small life.

It was only a neighborhood Catholic church; even so, Harry entered it with some trepidation, the training of his childhood still strong. If you were Jewish, such a thing was a sin; like all terrible sins it was likely to provoke a clap of thunder and a bolt of lightning from Jehovah, Who would strike a boy dead for defying His law, Thou shalt have no other God before me. Never mind that the

Catholic claimed their God was the same as the God of Moses. Who are you going to trust, the Pope or your rabbi? The rabbi said you would be struck by lightning, the Pope in Rome said you would be eternally saved. If the Pope was so smart, why were half the immigrants in New York Italians?

Inside the church a few parishioners were in prayer, the six-o'clock Mass presided over by an elderly priest. Harry moved quietly down the aisle, his hat in his hand, until he found her. Mrs. Rahner was on her knees, her head bowed in prayer. Harry moved to her and knelt beside her.

"Mrs. Rahner?" he whispered.

She turned to look at him. Her eyes widened in anger. To think he would intrude *here*!

"You are not welcome," she said.

"He's my God, too." Even the Pope admitted that.

Mrs. Rahner turned her back to him.

"Bess has been trying to reach you," Harry said. "She's in the hospital. She lost our child."

"God's will." Coldly.

"She's very sick. All she wants is to see you. She's still a little girl."

"You tell Beatrice I will never see her again."

"You're still her mother."

"No, I'm not. She married a Jew, she takes the consequences. Now please go."

Some of the other worshippers had turned to
watch, annoyed.

"I'm not leaving until you come with me," Harry
said. "I promised her."

"Never."

"Please."

"Shhhh. Can't you see we're at prayer?"

"I'm praying, too."

He put on his hat.

"Take off that hat!"

"I'm sorry, my father taught me to put it on."

Now the priest was looking up, the Vespers interrupted. He cleared his throat, to get their attention.

Harry, very softly, started to pray, in Hebrew.
Mrs. Rahner found herself the focus of the eyes
of the congregation as he continued. She flushed,
angrily, not knowing how to manage this.

"What are you saying?" she whispered, aware
the priest's eyes were upon her.

"I'm saying Kaddish, Mrs. Rahner. It's the prayer
for the dead. I'm saying it for you."

The priest had returned to his prayerbook. A
fierce whisper interrupted him again, and as he
looked up, the entire congregation was turning to
watch.

Mrs. Rahner was leading Harry up the aisle,
pausing only to reach up and snatch the hat off
his head.

Harry's reply was to put his arm about her and usher her through the doors of her church and out into the real world.

## ACT THREE

~~~~~~~~~~~~~~~

IN the New World, the ancient practice of arrang-
ing proper marriages between sons and daughters,
a business much too important to be left to children, was slipping out of the hands of the immigrant
parents. A new sense of freedom, a new kind of
liberty, words such as "love" and "romance," were
entering into the arrangements, and with them, of
course, another exciting new word, "divorce."

Mrs. Weiss had lost one son to a *shiksa*. She was
overjoyed that another son, Nathan, was marrying
a nice Orthodox girl named Sarah. Sarah was a
hot-eyed Jewish princess, she went to temple, she
had a good dowry; how could Cecilia know that
eventually Sarah would wind up sleeping with her
son Leo? And would divorce Nathan to do it? She
had wanted a daughter-in-law with a *tuchas*, she

got one. It almost destroyed the family.

But at the wedding in the crowded little apartment, all of this was in the future, almost as distant as men walking on the moon. There were the comfortably familiar elements, the *schnapps*, the honey cake, the hot tea, the pickled herring, the wedding *chupa* under which the couple were married, the glass ground under the foot of the rabbi, the laughter and tears and the singing and the *hora*, danced by all the guests, young and old, ringing the happy couple in the center. As each of her sons kissed the blushing bride, Cecilia didn't notice the gleam in the beautiful Sarah's eye, the look of a hungry virgin suddenly confronted with her first smorgasbord. A nice Jewish girl? Perhaps.

Bess sat at the battered piano playing the lively melody for the dancing, wearing a bathrobe, her face still pale and drawn. She had insisted on staying up—wasn't this also New Year's Eve? Perhaps the laughter would help soothe the ache inside her. Perhaps not.

Mrs. Rahner stood beside her, disapproving everything except the glass of *schnapps* in her hand. She had not wanted to come, but Bess had insisted that if the two families were to become friends, her mother couldn't ignore such an occasion.

"You shouldn't be up so late," her mother told Bess. "You're not well yet."

"I'm all right. How often does one of Harry's brothers get married?"

"From the way the bride's acting, she thinks she's honeymooning with all of them."

"Oh, Ma, don't be so *goyish*."

Mrs. Rahner stared at her daughter.

"My God," she said.

Harry pulled Mrs. Weiss into the center of the dancers, as the wedding guests began to clap the infectious rhythm, faster and faster, everyone a little *shicker*. Cecilia had to force herself to keep up the tempo, the *hora* becoming a challenge, Harry urging her on, until finally she collapsed in his arms, breathless, laughing, aching, but happy.

"Thank God," she panted, "I only got one more son to get married!" She turned to the bride, but she spoke loud enough for Bess, at the piano, to hear.

"You should have a dozen babies, all of them boys, all of them Orthodox, we'll have a dozen circumcisions!"

Everyone laughed, but Harry saw Bess suddenly get to her feet, and run for the bedroom.

"Bess!" he shouted, and ran after her, but she slammed the door in his face. He opened it and started in, everyone talking at once now, what did you expect, she's a *shiksa,* you heard about the baby? Shhh, shah, not so loud.

Mrs. Rahner noticed Mrs. Weiss pushing her way through the guests.

"She's a sick girl," Mrs. Rahner called out. "If he's not out in five minutes, I'm going in there!"

"I did that once. Didn't help," Mama told her, remembering.

Bess had thrown herself on the brass bedstead, her face buried in the pillows, as her husband stood by, helpless to comfort her.

"She shouldn't have said that." Harry seated himself on the bed. "Sometimes she doesn't think." He patted her. She pushed his hand away. "Come on, it's New Year's Eve, it's Nathan's wedding, it's time to have fun!"

Slowly, Bess turned herself over to face him.

"I talked to the doctor today. So did your mother."

"I know, she told me, the doctor said you're fine."

"I'm wonderful. I'm perfect. Except for one little thing. I lost our baby. Now I can't have any more, ever."

"*Never*? He said *that*?"

"It's all right, your mother is very happy."

She rolled over again, helplessly, forlornly. A child, Harry thought, a little girl who had given up pretending to be grown up. Something she had wanted so much had been snatched away from her, and there was no way, in a whole lifetime, to get it back. It wasn't much she had wanted. Immortality.

He looked around, remembering. He had meant to bring them to her in the hospital, but he had forgotten. Or perhaps he felt in the hospital it would have been too sentimental. He opened the drawer and handed her the package.

"I got you a New Year's present."

She didn't answer. He unwrapped it for her and opened the lid and the little music box started to play.

"Rosabelle, sweet Rosabelle . . ."

What child could resist? Slowly, Bess sat up to take it in her hand.

"That's not all," Harry said, and reached into the air. "Presto change-o!"

In his fingers rested a gold wedding band. She dropped the music box, a little girl no longer.

"Harry! Real gold?"

"Solid. The one Nathan bought is only plated. I don't think his wife is genuine, either."

Bess took the ring from him. They both knew there was no way he could afford it. The act had been canceled after the disaster in Bridgeport.

"Where did you get the money?"

"Just read the engraving."

She held the ring up to the light. Inside, the engraved words ran all the way around, elegantly inscribed in the gold. She read them, slowly.

"I'm going to cry again."

Harry took the ring and slipped it on her finger. Too tight, she noted, maybe I'll have to take it back and have it sized. I hope it's paid for, she thought, through the tears.

"You tell anyone what it says, I'll deny it," Harry said. "Now get to bed."

He lifted her to her feet and started to remove her robe.

"Harry, where did you get the money?"

"I sold the act, all the props and everything. Never take it off, you hear? As long as you live."

He had tried to say it quickly, maybe she hadn't noticed, he didn't want to talk about it.

She stared at him in disbelief.

"You mean I'm wearing the whole act on my finger? I don't want it!"

She started to pull it off, but it stuck, and Harry grabbed her hand.

"Not the whole act. I paid the hospital bill, too."

"How could you sell the act?"

"It wasn't easy—everybody read the notices."

She knew what it must have meant to him. Unreasonably, her reaction was anger. It was just like him, to try to take the spotlight away. To spoil their sweetest moment by pulling the rug from under her.

"Harry, don't do this for me. I'll hate myself."

"I'm doing it for me. You think I like being the biggest flop in show business? I got myself a great job in the tie factory, they say I'm the best cutter they ever had. Every time I finish a tie I take a bow."

"The tie factory?" She couldn't believe it. "With two dozen stinking old men?"

Harry shrugged.

"Maybe they'll wash."

She knew now. It was all clear.

"Tell the truth, Harry. Mama made you do it. Didn't she? *Didn't* she?"

She tried to pull the ring off her finger, loathing it, loathing everything it stood for.

"You take off that ring, I'll hate you!" He grabbed for her, and she pulled out of his grasp.

"Don't touch me! Don't ever touch me again!"

"Bess!"

"Don't come near me!"

And she was out the door, into the living room, pushing the guests aside. They were waltzing to "The Blue Danube," she remembered later. She shoved them aside as Harry raced after her. She was screaming, "I hate you! I hate you!" and her nightgown was flapping about her ankles. She could hear the chorus of "Oy vays!" as she disappeared into the kitchen and slammed the door behind her and leaned against it to catch her breath.

Harry pounded on the door a moment, then he kicked it open.

"Open, Sesame," Theo called out. There was embarrassed laughter, and Harry disappeared into the kitchen.

"Everybody have some honeycake," Mrs. Weiss said loudly, her reflexes still operating, and started hastily after them.

Bess had retreated behind the kitchen table as

Harry attempted to reach her, to reason with her. Cecilia threw the door open.

"Ehrich? What's wrong?"

"Mama, leave us alone, this is private."

"So what's private from a mother?" She closed the door and it was immediately opened by Mrs. Rahner.

"Bess!" she cried. "What did he do to you?"

"Please," said Mrs. Weiss, "this is private!" And she closed the door in her face.

"You see? It's hopeless." Bess was still backing away from Harry.

"What's hopeless?" Mama asked.

"Bess thinks you made me sell the act."

Bess whirled on her mother-in-law, glad to have the opportunity to transfer her anger.

"How could you do such a thing? It's Harry's whole life!"

And she put her arms around him. Harry, a little bewildered by the oscillations of the feminine mind, seized the opportunity to declare a truce. He kissed her.

"I'll get over it," he said. "You're more important than any act."

Cecilia Weiss was watching him. So, the marriage wasn't breaking up. Yet. She could wait. In the meantime, there were fences to mend.

"You sold the magic?" she asked her *meshugeneh* son. "The goldfish and everything?" He made goldfish disappear from a bowl, that's what he had been doing for a living. You can imagine?

Harry stared at her.

"You knew I was going to. It wasn't much, you said so yourself."

"What do I know from an act? I'm an expert?" A strategic retreat.

"Mama, you never wanted your son to be a magician. So I took that job in the tie factory."

Here was the opening. Cecilia whirled on Bess, the target all the time.

"So! You see? This is what you make him do, a tie factory, to support a wife who can't even have his children!"

"Harry, don't let her twist things around!"

"You're going to let a *shiksa* call your own mother a liar?"

"Shhh! Shah! Both of you!" How had he wound up in the middle? "Mama, it was my idea. How do you think I feel? Theo's in business, Nathan's a lawyer, Leo's in medical school. What am I?"

She looked at her son and her heart went out to him. A wife, a family, he was too young, he was different, he was ready to throw everything away, for what? Fortunately, he had a mother who understood, who loved him, who would help him overcome the terrible mistake of his marriage. She crossed and touched his face.

"What are you, Ehrincha?" She shrugged theatrically. Mama had never been on the stage. She probably had missed her calling.

"I remember," she said. "I remember when you were a child only, your poor father may he rest in peace, died, we all went to the cemetery, at the grave you wanted to jump in and help him get out." She touched his face again. "A doctor you're not. A lawyer you're not. What are you, Ehrich, I don't know, but I want you should try to be it."

"What I want to be, nobody wants. I been to every booking office in town. The Great Houdini couldn't get a job following Fink's Mules."

He sank into a chair. He could open any lock he ever saw—not through chance, through knowledge. He had spent years studying them, taking them apart, learning their principles. With a tiny "feke," a pick lock made of steel wire, he could feel his way inside a keyhole and make it give up its secrets. A strip of spring steel could be forced into a doorlock, springing it, if you knew just how. Harry knew. He could dive into freezing cold water and open a pair of handcuffs underwater—if they contained no birdshot—because he had Bess carry cakes of ice to him in the bathtub where he conditioned his body, night after night, when they were lucky enough to have a bathtub. It was a passion. It was insanity. He was a *meshugeneh*. And what was his reward? He was the best tie cutter on Rivington Street.

"All your friends say you should go to Europe, it'll be different." Until now, Bess hadn't wanted to mention it. She had wanted to stay home, to domesticate him, to live a normal married life with her husband. But the doctor had just told her a normal married life was impossible. And did she really want to see this strange man she had married domesticated? Pacing his barred cage, when he could spring the lock in seconds if she gave him the feke?

"What's in Europe?" Mama wanted to know. It was the first she had heard it mentioned.

"Nothing," Harry said.

"More theaters," Bess told her, "bigger audiences, it's easier to get a start. And once they want you in Europe, they want you twice as much over here."

It was true. The young country still had an inferiority complex. Performers who had played in Europe had snob appeal. There were ads in the theatrical weeklies, "Foreign Baggage Labels, 50¢. Fool your friends." And theater managers. Possibly yourself.

"You want to go?" Mrs. Weiss asked him.

"More than anything in the world," Bess told her.

"Let me hear it from him."

Harry shrugged.

"Who needs it?"

He wants it this much? Mrs. Weiss knew her son. She crossed to the flour bin near the sink and opened it. Bess had started to remove her wedding ring.

"Harry, this ought to pay part of the passage to Europe and—"

He grabbed her hand and held the ring fast. "I only made the down payment," he confessed. "It wouldn't take us past Hoboken."

From underneath the flour, Mrs. Weiss pulled the Mason jar. The Bank of England, King Solomon's Mines, Tutankhamen's tomb, all the repositories of treasure of the past, never held the wealth hidden in a hundred thousand Mason jars in the flour bins of immigrant mothers. The work, the pain, the deceit that was entailed in gathering the coins and the bills together and keeping their existence secret outweighed the worth of the gold of the Indies. Who could trust banks? Who could trust their own flesh and blood? Who would ever put hands in the flour except mama? Safe, from a greedy world, safe, the only real friend a Jewish family ever had.

She didn't want her son to go away from her. But the farthest he could travel was to the side of his wife. This would help keep him home, no matter where the *shiksa* took him. She blew the flour off the jar and unscrewed the top and poured out onto the table the pennies and nickels and quarters and dollar bills and fives and tens that she had put away, so carefully, for so many years.

"I was saving to buy a headstone," she said. "Who needs it? When I die, everybody will know who I am, the Great Houdini's mother. That's not bad." She shook the bills off, straightened them out, and held them out to her son.

"For Europe. Take it, Ehrich."

"Take it, Harry," Bess said.

"Please, you should stay off my side," Cecilia told her daughter-in-law, and the old clock, the clock from Budapest, began to strike midnight, and the new generation at the Jewish wedding in the other room started to sing a song written by a Scotchman, can you imagine, a Scotchman?

*"Should auld acquaintance be forgot*
*An' never brought to mind—"*

From outside, from the streets of New York's East Side, came the noise, spoons pounding on pots, lids pounding on lids—who would spend money for something to make noise with when everything around made noise? It was time to welcome the New Year, it had to be better than the old year; bang the kettles, shout the news, the old year is dead, may it go to Hell!

Harry knew what the money in the jar had cost her. He put his arms around his mother and held her to him.

"All right, Mama. I'll take it. But I'll send for you. Soon as I'm a hit, I'll send for you. The relatives should drop dead, I'll make you the Queen of Budapest!"

She clung to him, her battle won.

"Personally, Ehrich," she said, "I prefer Paris."

He laughed, and threw open the ice-covered window to the freezing wind and the deafening noise, as the East Side greeted its future.

"Listen, Mama—1900!" He kissed her. "It's the Twentieth Century!"

"Only outside," Bess said. But no one heard her.

The whole family came down to see them off, most of them carrying food. They thought it was like when you came over in the steerage—who thought there would be a regular dining room aboard?

Mama was in tears as she waved goodbye. Harry ran down the gangplank three times to console her, to promise her again he would send for her. Bess watched from the deck, keeping her thoughts to herself.

The ship pulled out into the harbor, the tugboats struggled to move her into the tide, then she swung around and they cast off the lines and the huge steamer was alone against the ocean, just like me, thought Bess.

They had no engagement set. No agent. They would go to London. Harry was certain they would get bookings; all they had to do was audition. They would open in England and the notices would bring the European managers running.

Bess didn't want to dampen his enthusiasm, she

just hoped she wouldn't lock herself in the trunk again.

Harry spent most of the voyage in his bunk, deathly seasick, and they were both relieved to see the British coastline, feeling the worst was over.

# ACT FOUR

NO ONE had heard of the Great Houdinis in London, which might have been fortunate, but no one *wanted* to hear about them. The booking agents were wary of American acts. They had just been victimized by the Bullet Proof Man, an American who claimed to have supernatural powers to turn aside bullets fired from a revolver. The newspapers discovered his jacket and his pants were lined with ground glass and the cartridges had been tampered with to hold only a quarter-charge. Then there was the Georgia Magnet, a young lady who defied five strong men to lift her from the stage. Her Magnetic Power proved to be a knowledge of the principles of leverage and a liaison with four of the five. The fifth was a homosexual.

Unable to get a hearing, Harry spent much of his

time away from their boarding house visiting lock-
smiths to learn whatever he could about British
locks, British safes, British handcuffs. He discovered that the cuffs favored by the London police
looked formidable, but were of a type whose locking mechanism could be jarred loose with a sharp
blow. By wearing a piece of lead strapped to his
thigh beneath his trousers, he could spring them
easily.

What was more difficult was to get in to see
Dundas Slater, manager of the Alhambra Theatre
in London, the premier showcase for vaudeville in
those times. Day after futile day, Harry and Bess
sat in his outer office, waiting. The secretaries were
polite, but protective. Mr. Slater was occupied.
He had a conference. He was holding a meeting.
He was out of the city. He would not be back until
next week. But he always appeared, precisely at
noon, to cross the street to his favorite pub and
have a drink and a spot of lunch with one or two
of his cronies, looking neither to the right nor the
left as he passed through the office where half a
dozen hopefuls, including Bess and Harry, waited.

Harry's patience soon ran out. In only three
weeks, they had gone through Mama's headstone
and were starving again. The rent would soon be
due. He decided to beard the lion in his den. Harry
staked out a position at the bar in Shelley's Pub,
sharing a mug of lager with Bess, waiting for noon-
time. A barmaid carrying a huge tray of Scotch

salmon and tiny English sandwiches stopped with
the tray right under their noses, and Bess thought
she was going to faint. There had been no break-
fast that morning, and dinner the night before had
been tea and boiled potatoes.

The barmaid eyed the two of them with mistrust.
This was a posh saloon bar, and these two in their
unpressed American clothes hardly belonged.

"You been nursin' that pint 'arf an hour, luv,"
she told Harry. " 'Ave another or I'll be chargin'
rent."

"No, thanks, luv," Harry said, a little nervously.
"We're waiting for someone."

"Well, while you're waitin', that's thruppence
you owe me for the lager."

Harry reluctantly dug into his pocket and came
up with three lonely English pennies, their last
resource, and held them out to her. But as she
reached to take them, he closed his hand and
quickly opened it again. The pennies had disappeared.

" 'Ere now!" cried the barmaid, impressed.
" 'Ow in 'ell did you manage that?"

Harry closed his hand and opened it again. The
pennies were back. While her attention was
diverted, he flicked two sandwiches off her tray
in Bess's direction. She caught them in her opened
purse and closed it quickly, in practiced fashion.

The barmaid hadn't noticed.

"Bloody marvelous, that," she said, but she was referring to the pennies.

"And you're a bloody 'andsome lass, luv," Harry said, mimicking her accent. " 'Ow about puttin' the thruppence on the 'ouse?"

"Up yer bloody arse, Yank," she told him pleasantly, and grabbed the money before it could disappear again.

"Harry, it's twelve-thirty," Bess whispered. "He can't be coming in today. Let's go into the park and eat these sandwiches before I faint."

"Shhh! Here he comes!"

She turned to look. C. Dundas Slater, pompous, somewhat paunchy, ruddy-faced and well dressed, was entering the pub, deep in conversation with two companions, one distinguished-looking and mustachioed, the other somewhat older, taller, extremely British.

Harry took Bess by the arm and started to pull her through the dedicated drinkers about the bar.

"Remember," he told her, "we're headliners. One hundred pounds a week, that's our salary."

"A hundred pounds! That's five hundred dollars!"

"Right. Take it or leave it."

"Suppose he leaves it?"

"For an encore, we commit suicide."

"Harry, why don't we just ask for twenty dollars a week, like always?"

"Never. I'd rather die first. But if he won't pay five hundred, we'll take it."

He grinned at her. She tried to smile, but she was shaking again, and hunger was gnawing at her.

"Mr. Slater?" They had reached the booth, and the theater manager was looking up at them, annoyed, interrupted in the middle of his favorite anecdote about the Queen. It seems she and Prince Albert had once been in bed together at Buckingham when—

"And who might you be?" he inquired suspiciously of the strangely dressed young man who seemed vaguely familiar. The fool had interrupted Queen Victoria in a rare moment of tenderness.

"My card, sir," said Harry, and with a gesture, seemingly plucked a dozen business cards out of the air and deposited them on the table in front of the three Englishmen. The tall one and the one with the mustache seemed pleasantly impressed.

"The Great Houdinis?" inquired the tall one, picking up one of the cards and holding it to the light.

"The greatest magic act in the history of the business."

"Indeed?" The mustache smiled at his modesty.

"Top billing, every circuit in America," Harry continued, certain none of these well-dressed gentlemen would have deigned to visit the Colonies.

"Never heard of you," Slater said impatiently. He dealt with egos larger than this every day of his life. "Why don't you see me at the theater?"

At that, Bess became Bess again. The fear and

the hunger vanished. Here was a stupid man; she
had to charge forward, recklessly.

"That's what we've been trying to do, Mr. Slater!"
Harry motioned her to be quiet but Hell hath no
fury. "We've been sitting in your outer office for a
week, you're always too damn busy to see us, but
you take two hours for lunch every day and you're
fat as a pig!"

Slater was too startled to answer for a moment.

"The lady is my wife, the greatest mindreader
in show business!" Harry announced, hoping to
change the subject.

"If she can read my mind," said C. Dundas
Slater, "she's no lady." He chortled, pleased, and
turned to his companions. "Rather good, what?
Eh?"

"Always the gentleman, Dundas." The mustache
was not amused.

"Gentleman enough to pick up the check," Slater
grumbled. He turned back to Harry and Bess. "Go,
go, be gone, I'll have you run in, the two of you.
And don't come back to my office, I'll have you
thrown out." The matter settled, he turned back
to his guests. "What'll it be?"

"Thought you'd never ask," said the tall one.
"I think I'll have a gin and Italian, for starters."

"Guinness for me," said the mustache. "Then,
probably, the oysters."

Slater had ostentatiously taken out his monocle
to peer at the blackboard on the bar.

"I believe I fancy the Scotch salmon," he announced.

Harry had had enough. He reached over and snatched the monocle out of Slater's eye.

"I fancy the lox myself," he said, "but I haven't had a decent meal in three days!"

"All Harry wants is an audition," Bess added.

Slater's complexion turned even ruddier.

"I'll see he gets one at the Old Bailey!" He motioned to the burly Irish bouncer, who was in conference nearby with the barmaid and a police officer.

"Mr. Ryan! Officer!"

"Is the gentleman annoying you, Mr. Slater?" Ryan inquired, solicitously. This was the pub's best customer.

"Indeed he is! Will you remove him, please, sir?"

The barmaid pointed to Bess indignantly.

"She's the one, worse than 'im, she is, 'ave a look in 'er 'and bag!"

The bobby extended his hand toward Bess.

"Let's have a look in the bag, ma'am."

Bess was frightened now, looking around, wildly, willing to do anything but open the incriminating purse. She made the mistake of trying to run, and Ryan grabbed her and hurled her into the booth.

"Take your goddam hands off my wife!" Harry shouted, and grabbed him by the shoulder to pull him away. Ryan turned, a lifetime of dealing with obstreperous drunks making this just part of the routine, and slugged Harry in the pit of the stomach. That usually finished an argument without breaking anything. The victim would go down, painfully, all the breath and will to fight knocked out of him.

Not this time. Harry hadn't budged an inch. He turned to the startled manager.

"I do that in the act," he explained, quietly. Then he turned back and tensed his stomach muscles again. His abdomen, from constant exercise, from training in the mechanism of escape which required the agility of a contortionist, was as hard as a board. He often challenged any member of the audience to take two punches at it, freely. It pleased his vanity to think that he was made of iron.

One day, it killed him.

But not today. He motioned the surprised and angry Irishman to try again.

"Go ahead," he said, "I'm auditioning."

Ryan looked worriedly at Slater. He might cripple this fool. Slater nodded to go ahead. Serve the bastard right. Ryan threw a left to Harry's stomach that should have knocked him to the floor. Harry merely grimaced, then unexpectedly planted a right to Ryan's jaw that staggered him into an adjoining table.

"*That* was an ad lib," Harry said to Slater, "but if you like it I'll keep it in."

"Harry!" Bess shouted, "watch out!"

But she was too late. The policeman threw his arms about Harry from the rear and with practiced ease, pinioned him in a full Nelson. Harry struggled, but he was helpless. The bobby stood well over six feet, Harry was six inches shorter. A Napoleonic complex is fine if you have the French army to back it up.

"Get the cuffs out of my pocket, Jim," the officer shouted to Ryan, who was climbing back to his feet, rubbing his jaw. More than willing, Ryan pulled the handcuffs free and snapped them firmly about Harry's wrists.

"Now, my bucko," said the policeman, "we'll see what game you two are playing." He pulled out his pad. The barmaid had snatched the handbag from Bess and now she opened it, shaking its contents onto the table.

"What's the loot?" inquired the bobby, pencil poised.

Slater's companions had been observing the scene, quietly outraged, their sympathies aroused by Bess's helplessness and beauty. Now the tall one examined the meager contents of her purse, spread on the table before them.

"She appears to have purloined two cucumber sandwiches," he announced, "and a pickle."

"Obviously, a Russian spy," deduced the mustache. "Officer, search her at once and find out where she is hiding the sour cream."

"Now, now," protested their host, "don't go soft

on me. The woman is obviously a criminal."

"My dear Slater." The tall one was annoyed. "The only criminal here is you. You have behaved like an utter boor."

The mustache turned to the bobby.

"Release that gentleman from the manacles," he said, indicating Harry.

"Immediately!" insisted his companion.

"And who in hell might you two be, beggin' your pardon, gentlemen?"

"Good Heavens," the mustache muttered. "I think I've written that dialogue."

"I am Superintendent Owen Melville of Scotland Yard. I doubt if you've heard of it," said the tall one." You are a bloody idiot. And this," he said, indicating the mustached man, "is my good friend Sir Arthur Conan Doyle, the creator of a fellow named Sherlock Holmes."

"This is not one of my good days," the policeman remarked thoughtfully, as he pulled out his keys. "Hold out the wrists, I'll take off the cuffs, Guvnor."

"Don't bother." Harry struck the inside of each cuff against the lead plate hidden beneath his trouser leg. They flew open as he knew they would.

He slipped them off his wrists and threw them on the table in front of Scotland Yard's Superintendent.

"Cheap British merchandise . . . sir," he said.

Bess had often felt that one of Harry's problems

as a performer was that he never knew when to get off. It was never more true than that afternoon in London. Having triumphed over Slater and the British police, having been invited to share a luxurious lunch, Harry couldn't leave well enough alone. He had to boast that he could not only get out of any British handcuffs, he could also escape from any British prison. He meant, of course, after he had carefully studied its layout and its locking mechanisms. Houdini never attempted anything he had not carefully assured himself in advance was possible. But, with Slater slyly goading him on, he guaranteed he could escape from a British jail cell with no assistance at all, and that he could do it that very afternoon.

"Even from Scotland Yard?" inquired Slater. This, he knew, could be arranged instantly, before this upstart had an opportunity to copy its keys or bribe its guards. The Yard had a group of cells in which suspects were detained briefly before being moved to more distant quarters. Harry, over his third beer, stated boldly it would be no problem. And he allowed Slater to maneuver him into a bet of fifty pounds—two hundred and fifty dollars, as Bess carefully pointed out later, in the hansom cab.

"Harry, how are you going to pay if you lose?" she asked fearfully, as the carriage rolled along the Embankment and through the gates of New Scotland Yard on Derby Street, for this was before the Yard moved to its more famous headquarters in Whitehall Palace.

"I'm not going to pay it." Harry smiled at her and patted her hand. "What are they gonna do, throw me in jail?"

She knew he wasn't as confident as he sounded. He had bet Slater the money against a week's engagement at the Alhambra, which he wanted desperately; but he had agreed to submit to a body search, and he had no advance notice of the type of handcuffs or lock that he would encounter. Failure meant the end of all their hopes. Slater would see to it that every theater manager in the British Isles and on the Continent would hear of it.

As Sir Arthur and Superintendent Melville conducted them through the corridors of the Yard to the detention cells, Bess managed to slip into her mouth the tiny key Harry had handed her. She sneezed, and a horrible thought crossed her mind. Suppose she swallowed it before she could pass it to him? There would go fifty pounds and their whole career into her stomach.

Some of the prisoners turned curiously as the strange procession marched past their cells, the jailer with his keys leading the way, the prison doctor bringing up the rear. The jail smelled dank and Dickensian. The bars were of iron, the walls of cement and brick, the locks massive. No one had ever escaped from these dread surroundings.

"Step inside, Mr. Houdini," said the superintendent politely as the jailer swung open the bars to the last cell. "We shall soon see who'll win this wager." And he smiled, amused at the presumption of the man.

Bess started to follow Harry in, but Superintendent Melville stopped her.

"Sorry, Madame, Mr. Houdini is to be stripped naked in here."

"It's all right," Bess said anxiously, "I've seen him naked, we're very friendly. I'm his wife."

"No, ma'am," said the superintendent, "you're his accomplice." And as Bess tried to kiss Harry farewell, he interposed his hand between their mouths with a knowing smile, and Bess almost swallowed the key.

"Sorry," he said. "No conjugal rights."

The bars clanked shut in Bess's face. Dundas Slater was rubbing his hands together with glee.

"Well, well," he gloated. "The Great Houdini has met his match, it appears."

"If you don't mind, sir." The doctor was indicating to Harry to remove his clothes.

"I'm all yours, doc," said Harry, with a confidence he didn't feel, and slapped him on the back. Fortunately, most British doctors wore jackets made of wool, in traditional black. In Harry's hand was a tiny pouch of the same material, and an even tinier fishhook, which held it suspended,

almost invisibly, on the doctor's back, as he conducted his investigation of Harry's body.

"Remember, it's a week's engagement at the Alhambra," Harry reminded Dundas.

"If you ever get out of *this* engagement, which
I doubt. And if you don't, you owe me fifty pounds.
Which I also doubt you have."

"I'll get out," Harry assured him. "I'm the
greatest escape artist in the world."

"Dear, dear," murmured Sir Arthur, "how American!"

The superintendent had taken from the jailer a
pair of formidable handcuffs, which he showed to
the others.

"Scotland Yard's finest," he declared. "No regu-
lation flimsies. These are the same cuffs that held
Harry Tyne, who murdered six of his mistresses.
You remember him, Arthur? Had a glorious time."

"If I get out of the cuffs, will you sign a letter
saying so, on Scotland Yard stationery?"

Inspector Melville laughed. "Heavens, yes. Immediately before I resign."

Bess stood watching, outside the bars, as the
doctor carefully completed his search of Harry's
body. Behind her, some of the prisoners craned to
get a look at the strange proceedings. Bess knew
about the tiny pouch. Suppose the others did too?

"Have you searched him thoroughly, doctor?"
Dundas Slater wanted to know.

"Every crevice. There is nothing on him the Lord didn't give him."

"Except his swollen head," boomed Slater, and laughed again at his wit.

"You're a good man, doc," Harry told the doctor, and slapped him on the back again, much to his annoyance. But Harry didn't care. He had recovered the pouch during the slap.

Sir Arthur had been observing the proceedings, making mental notes for possible future use, perhaps "The Case of the Naked Prisoner." He felt a great sympathy for the strange young man with his compulsion for danger.

"I'm rooting for you, old chap," he said, as they began to move out. "You're an authentic character."

"We shall lock this cell," the superintendent told Harry, "go to my office and have a spot of sherry, and return in exactly one hour—unless, of course, you give up sooner."

"Where's your office?" Harry wanted to know.

The superintendent appeared surprised.

"Why, it's beyond the cell area, through the barred gate, and across the reception room."

"I'll meet you there. Save me some sherry."

"Cheeky little bastard," said Dundas, and watched carefully as the jailer locked the cell and then brought down the steel bar that was attached to a padlock at the end of the corridor, out of reach of the prisoners, and formed a double locking system. Slater took Bess by the arm and steered her down the corridor past the silent prisoners.

She was trembling again. She knew about the pouch, but it contained only a tiny feke. Suppose it wouldn't work on the huge manacles? She glanced over her shoulder. Harry was waving at her. He seemed to be confident, but Harry would have looked confident going over Niagara Falls in a doughnut. The *meshugeneh*, she thought. My God, Mama's got *me* saying it.

Harry waited until he heard the barred door clang at the end of the corridor. The prisoners, mangy, louse-ridden, hopeless, pressed against their bars to watch, silently. He suddenly realized this wasn't just a bet; he was a symbol, to these unfortunates, a symbol that authority could be defied and defeated. Up the Republic! Several of them were Irish.

Harry carefully opened his hand and showed them the tiny pouch in his palm. He took out the bit of metal, glinting in the half-light. Then he pressed two hands to the muscles of his throat. Thank God for the old Japanese in the circus, he thought, the one who could swallow a billiard ball and retain it in his throat to regurgitate later, as his partner struck a Chinese gong. He had taught Harry his pitiful secret, and now Harry thanked him, silently, as from the back of his throat he produced the telescoped metal extension, only a few inches long, which when opened could reach more than half a yard.

The tiny feke fitted into the lock of the handcuffs, but it would only turn the release a short way. Desperately, Harry yanked at the cuffs, open now only a notch or two, but they would not budge. He could hear the hard breathing of the prisoners, crouching to see better between their bars, silently rooting for him, as he wet his wrists with his mouth and exerted his tremendous strength. Both his wrists were bleeding badly as he finally managed to get loose from the manacles.

But the battle had only begun. The lock at the end of the cell corridor was beyond the reach of his arms. Naked, he sat on the cold floor of the jail cell and opened the extension to its full length. The feke fitted into the end of it. He placed the extension between the big toe and the second toe of his right foot, clung to the bars, and extended his foot toward the padlock. It just barely reached. He tried to get the feke into the keyhole. He missed. He tried again. No use. And again.

Some of the prisoners were sweating now, working as hard as Harry. If one man could escape, if any man could escape, the victory was theirs as well as his.

In his comfortable office, paneled in fine wood, filled with Victorian desks and chairs and a couch which would later become kitsch but was now the epitome of modern design, Superintendent Melville was pouring Spanish sherry into exquisite cut glasses. Bess had already nervously downed three drinks, hoping against hope to pass out, while Dundas Slater was expounding on his favorite theme.

"Bluff, sheer bluff," he insisted. "The cheek of some of these performers is amazing. You wouldn't believe the number I turn away every day before—"

He was interrupted by feminine screams, horrified sounds from the next room.

"What the devil?" The superintendent was across the room in a bound, throwing open the door, committing the unpardonable sin of spilling good sherry on the carpeting.

His secretaries, two of them, were standing behind their desks, screaming loudly as they covered their eyes. As he shouted to them for an explanation, they pointed beyond the glass partition.

Harry Houdini, stark naked, was unlocking the barred gate from the cell corridor with the tiny feke. He stepped through and locked it behind him, seemingly oblivious to the fact that all his clothing was in the doctor's custody, in the superintendent's office.

As he saw Melville and the others frozen in the doorway, he waved to them happily.

"Ah, superintendent!" he called. "How about a drink for my friends?"

And down the stairway bounded the prisoners he

had released, whistling, jeering, free men at last behind the barred gate, even though only in spirit.

But what is more important than that?

## ACT FIVE

~~~~~~~~~~

"THE GREAT HOUDINI," read the marquee at the Alhambra, "VICTOR OVER SCOTLAND YARD!"

Dundas Slater was a man of his word. He was also a smart businessman. The story was all over London in a few hours, and he cashed in on it, swallowing his pride in favor of his wallet. Overnight, Harry had made it to the top of the bill. The act's salary became sixty pounds per week, and the engagement was extended again and again, for six full months. Harry had discovered the key to an audience—the challenge, with a price tag. He allowed himself to be shut into packing cases, safes, butter churns, mailbags, always announcing an award, a hundred pounds or better, for any restraint that could hold him.

His fame spread to the Continent and he was in demand everywhere. After London he was booked into the Central Theater in Dresden, and eventually graduated to the Wintergarten in Berlin. He leaped into German rivers, manacled hand and foot, and always came up free. The German police became fearful. He escaped from their handcuffs, from their jails. In the Europe of those times, especially in Germany, any challenge to the police was a challenge to the government. The common man, fearful, controlled, was being shown a bad example, disrespect for authority. How could decent government exist without shackles?

Harry Houdini was hauled into court by the German police, charged with misrepresentation. He had stated publicly he could escape from any restraint; the truth was he could not escape from the manacles of the German State Police. In the courtroom, Harry called for their shackles. With the public barred, he demonstrated to the judge how easily he could free himself. He was acquitted of the charge. The police, outraged, appealed to a higher court, and again Harry performed in a cleared courtroom, and escaped. It was too dangerous to let him go on. Who knows, he might find a way to escape from Germany itself. He was declared innocent, and promptly had handbills and posters printed proclaiming, "The Imperial Police of Cologne were compelled to publicly advertise 'An Honorary Apology' to Harry Houdini, by command of Kaiser Wilhelm II, Emperor of Germany."

The next stop was Moscow. Not as in the past, Moscow, Idaho, but Moscow, Russia, then a swinging capital if you were of the upper classes. All the top acts in the world played there, the money was good, the applause plentiful. But it was gaiety on top of a volcano. Harry noted in his diary the numbers of prisoners he saw being herded through the streets to the prison vans, drawn by horses, which would carry them to Siberia. The vans were sealed tightly except for a small barred window through which food was passed. There were no sanitary facilities. After the endless journey, the prisoners were hauled out and the van was flushed down with buckets of water.

Troubled, Harry and Bess went onstage to perform before a bejeweled audience that had barely heard of them. Harry insisted on addressing them in Russian, which he claimed to have learned from the immigrants on New York's East Side. It was a catastrophe. The Russian he thought he was speaking turned out to be Polish with a heavy Yiddish accent, and the audience began shouting at them, jeering. It was East Hartford all over again, and the entire engagement was endangered.

Something had to be done to retrieve the situation. Harry at once thought of his success with Scotland Yard. The Russian equivalent was the Czar's Secret Police. But Chief Lebedev was no Inspector Melville; never would he allow anyone to attempt an escape from a Russian prison, at a time when so many were trying. He had heard of Houdini's exploits in London; of course, such a thing could not be accomplished in *his* prisons, but he would be a fool to allow anyone to try.

As a last resort, Harry asked to be allowed to escape from a *carette,* the van that transported the condemned to Siberia. Lebedev grinned. He knew something he felt certain Harry didn't know: a *carette* was lined with steel, and the key that locked it in Moscow could not unlock it; that key was in Siberia. He gave the Great Houdini permission to attempt to escape, provided he did it naked, after a thorough search, and while the *carette* was inside the walls of the courtyard of Lubianka Prison.

Bess pleaded with Harry not to try. The conditions were too difficult, there was no opportunity for him to inspect one of the vans and check out the locking mechanism, failure would only compound their difficulties in Russia. And success might have the same effect. It was difficult enough getting into Russia. If he humiliated the Secret Police, getting out might be even more dangerous. The minute she said it, Bess was sorry. It only made Harry more determined. Jews were not admitted to Czarist Russia; Bess had filled out their religious certificates attesting they were Roman Catholics.

"You've given back my circumcision!" Harry had shouted at her, but she had insisted it was the only way they could fulfill the engagement. No one had to tell Harry that many of the inmates of the *carettes* were of his own faith; the faces of those who gathered to see the vans start off, the very atmosphere of Moscow itself, made that unmistakable. With him, escape was a game. To the Jews of Russia, it was life or death. All of them were fiddlers on a roof, waiting for it to cave in beneath them, as it seldom failed to do. Perhaps Russian officialdom didn't know he was Ehrich Weiss, son of a rabbi. He was certain the underground knew. If he got out, word would spread to ten thousand beleaguered Tevyes.

Inside the prison walls, Harry was stripped naked and subjected to the most severe body search of his career, by men who performed that duty every day of their lives. His only assistance came from Bess, and from Franz Kukol, a young Austrian who had become his assistant, and was to remain with him until World War I, and a prior loyalty, broke up their association.

Harry was locked, naked, inside the steel-lined van, the Moscow weather a freezing 21 degrees. The story is that he struggled for an hour and a half to find a way out, to reach the padlock through the tiny barred window and find some way to force it open. It was also said that Bess passed to him, in a kiss, a coil of clock-spring metal with its edge notched into saw teeth, which could hacksaw through cold steel.

He got out. At the end of an hour and a half,

through the door of the van which was hidden by a corner of a building from his captors' gaze, Harry Houdini made his escape, dripping with perspiration despite the teeth-chattering temperature, only to be seized by the Russian Secret Police, who subjected him to a complete body search again and found nothing.

He never revealed how he had accomplished it, except to remark, later, that in Holy Russia, the most powerful weapon of escape was a hundred-ruble note, carefully inserted between the fingers of a jailer.

However it was done, Lebedev was outraged. He refused to sign the letter he had promised, and declined to allow any report of the incident in the press. He knew what it would cost him: either his job, or his head. And he was attached to both.

But Harry had figured correctly. His people knew. They knew almost instantly who he was, what he had done, and why. And the word spread, contagiously, through a society crying out for change. Suddenly, crowds appeared at the theater, such crowds as had never been seen before. Harry and Bess played four solid months in Moscow, at three different theaters, and left only to play at the Nischni-Novgorod Fair, whose beginnings went back to 1366, in the Ural Mountains, on the route to Siberia.

Everywhere Harry went in Russia, he was not just the Great Houdini.

He was Ehrich Weiss, who had escaped.

Paris was a relief after the tensions of Moscow. Harry arranged for seven bearded Parisians, wearing top hats, to sit at a sidewalk table outside Fouquet's on the Champs Élysée. Every time a pretty girl went by—in Paris, that would be every five seconds—the men would doff their hats simultaneously, revealing painted on seven bald pates the letters H-O-U-D-I-N-I. *Gauche,* the French called it, but they all went to the theater to see this American *maître* of bad taste.

It was their honeymoon, the first time they had been able to relax together, to sample the fine food of the *haute cuisine*, to wander the *Rive Gauche* between shows, to stare at Gustave Eiffel's tower, built for the Exhibition of 1889 and still the subject of controversy. Was it beautiful? Was it ugly? Would it fall over?

Only the language was a problem for Bess, a problem magnified by Harry's ease with any tongue —except Russian and Polish, which he somehow found interchangeable.

The first time they performed the Metamorphosis before a Parisian audience, Bess almost destroyed it. Harry was inside the locked trunk, Bess was in tights with French ruffles, looking charming. The orchestra was playing "Rosabelle." The theater was ornately Parisian, crowded to the top of the third balcony.

With a flourish, Bess began to close the drapes. "I draw the curtain like—"

From inside the trunk came Harry's voice, a tense whisper.

"For Christ's sake, in French, in French!"

Bess looked at the trunk hopelessly.

"Harry, I forgot the words."

The orchestra continued to play, happily drowning out their whispers.

"*Je tire le rideau comme ça.*"

"Oh, my God," said Bess.

Harry groaned and tried again.

"*Je tire . . .*" he began.

"*Je tire,*" Bess called out, loudly enough and badly enough for the first ten rows of Frenchmen to cringe.

"*. . . le rideau . . .*"

"*Le rideau . . .*"

"*. . . comme ça!*"

"*Comme ça!*"

"Mazeltov," came Harry's voice from within the trunk. Happily relieved, Bess pulled the curtains shut, clapped her hands three times, and mercifully disappeared.

Harry threw the curtains open, free of the locked trunk and the manacles.

"*Et voilà* Le Grand Houdini!" he shouted, waiting for the applause.

It came in waves, and continued and continued. The audience didn't want to give Bess another opportunity to mangle the most beautiful language in Europe.

A small story in the London *Times* carried the announcement:

### Houdini Returns to London
### After Continental Tour

Few noticed it, because this was the issue of the *Times* bordered in black to announce the passing of Victoria, Queen of the United Kingdom of Great Britain and Ireland, Empress of India, granddaughter of George III, daughter of Edward, Duke of Kent and Princess Victoria Mary Louisa of Saxe-Coburg-Gotha. Queen Victoria had worn the crown for sixty-three years, and had given her name to an unforgettable era of solid furniture and solid families. When her beloved Albert had died, she wrote her uncle Leopold, who happened to be King of the Belgians, "I am *determined* that no one person is to lead or guide or dictate *to me*. Though miserably weak and utterly shattered, my spirit rises when I think *any* wish or plan of Albert's is to be touched or changed, or I am to be *made to do* anything." Miserably weak and utterly shattered, she ruled for thirty-nine firm years after Albert's death, and not even Disraeli could *make her do* anything she didn't want to. Only God, eventually, succeeded, and there is some question as to whether He asked her permission first.

The period of mourning for the Queen didn't interfere with the opening of the Great Houdinis at the Empire. After all, Victoria would have insisted that business continue as usual. Business, in her eyes, was Britain. Rule, Britannia. And keep the shops open nights.

On an unusual sunny day that winter, Harry and Bess drove in an open carriage down London's streets toward their theater. Bess knew the reason for the open carriage, despite the cold: Harry had gotten that old star feeling and wanted an opportunity to wave to his subjects. He was wearing an expensive coat with a fur collar, a scarf knotted at his neck and fastened with a jeweled stickpin, and in his hand he held a cane which he occasionally raised in acknowledgment to any of the passersby who recognized him, and a few who didn't. Never mind. They soon would. Bess was wearing one of her unobtrusive cloth coats and would have been happier in a warm hansom cab; she watched Harry's enjoyment without comment. The performer's mentality was something she understood, but didn't want. Applause for the sake of applause, ego for the sake of ego, the need for an audience at all times, those to her were affectation, while to Harry Houdini they were bread and butter.

Bess put up with him until, at one point, he raised a monocle to his eye to survey his public, royally. She snatched it from his hand and stared through it.

"Plate glass," she announced. "Lord Ehrich Weiss, of Coney Island."

Harry grabbed the monocle back. It had taken him half an hour to learn to hold it in his eye.

"We're a hit now," he told her. "We gotta act like one. Why are you wearing that old dress?"

Bess looked at her dress, beneath the cloth coat. It was plain, but serviceable.

"Because you bought it for me," she said.

"I gave you plenty of money to buy a new one."

"It's not the same thing."

He was waving the cane again, and barely heard her. Or if he heard, barely understood.

"You've got to stop being small-time." He placed the monocle in his eye again. "The trick is to be noticed." He waved. "Get into the headlines. It's more important than the act."

They had entered a business area now, the street lined with elegant shops.

"Poor Harry. You're jealous of Queen Victoria because she thought of dying before you did, and you can't figure out a way to top that."

"I already have."

"How?"

"By being the first one to come back."

"Second, Harry, second."

He grinned at her. "You go to your church, I'll go to mine."

She shook her head helplessly.

"I'll bet you'll do it, too, just to take a bow."

"No," he said, "to see you again."

A shock passed through her. Somehow she knew he meant it. When he tried to kiss her, she pushed him away.

"Stop it," she said. "I'm trying to stay mad at you."

A shop window caught his eye and he called to the driver to stop.

"Bess, look at that!"

She had never seen a dress so beautiful in her life. Victoria, after the passing of Albert, had refused to wear color of any sort. This dress was black, but it was black lace, and it was sequined, elegant. It stood alone, on a form, in the center of the huge show window. An unostentatious card beside it told the story: Designed for Her Majesty Before the Sad Event.

They were out of the carriage now, Harry leading her to the window; she stood in front of it, enthralled.

"Oh, Harry! It's absolutely gorgeous!"

"Do you think it would fit Mama?" he asked.

She stood at the top of the stairway of the Royal Hotel in Budapest, an old lady who had left the country countless years ago with only the clothes on her back; now her dress had been designed for the greatest Queen of her century.

"It's too tight, I can't breathe," Mama said.

Her *meshugeneh* son had rented the entire ball-room of the grandest hotel in Budapest and brought his mother all the way from East 69th Street to give her this moment, in front of all the relatives— Uncle Heller, the family aristocrat who had fought her marriage to that penniless rabbi Maier Weiss, the aunts, the nephews, the nieces, all of them here at the bottom of the great staircase, sipping cham-pagne as if they liked it, whispering to each other what they knew was the truth: it was taking Harry's last penny to make this impression on them. So, they would try not to look impressed.

Mama hesitated. She clutched Harry's right arm. Bess was on his left.

"Maybe I should go back upstairs," Mama said fearfully.

Harry laughed. "Mama, I love you." He kissed her, so the guests could see. "All my life you've been telling me you wanted to come back and show off for the relatives, and now you're afraid."

He started to lead them down the stairs, proudly, his two women. Could it be he really didn't under-stand? At the last moment, Cecilia Weiss broke away.

"No," she said, "you'll excuse, I can't."

She turned and started back up the stairs. Harry ran after her.

"What's wrong, Mama?"

She turned and looked at him.

"You don't know?"

He shook his head. Everyone was staring. She would have to explain, he was a child.

"We left here," she said, slowly, "we were nothing, but your father was a rabbi in the temple, a religious man, to him everybody looked. The first time in thirty-years, how can I hold up my head, my daughter is a *shiksa*? The relatives are laughing behind their face." She was pleading with him now, her voice strained, close to breaking. "Send her upstairs, don't do this to me, Ehrich, don't do this."

Bess was waiting. The relatives were trying to listen.

"Mama, Bess is my wife." Wasn't a man allowed to belong to two women, if one was his mother? "I didn't bring her here to hide her. If you won't come down the stairs with us, we'll go alone."

Harry waited. Mama made no move. Slowly, deliberately, Harry turned and started down the steps toward his wife.

"Ehrich!"

He stopped.

"I'm an old *yenta*, don't walk so fast."

She moved down the steps to him. He smiled and took her arm, then he took Bess's, and the three of them descended the grand staircase of the Royal Hotel together.

Harry, being a man, foolishly thought he had won.

The relatives fought over each other to greet Cecilia, as if nothing were wrong, as if they weren't whispering about it at the same time that they crowded around, laughing, crying, kissing her. It would have been an emotional moment had they been only Hungarian, but they were both Hungarian and Jewish, and the ballroom echoed with their emotion until it almost drowned in *gemütlichkeit*.

Harry led Mama to the ornate chair, like a throne, that the manager had set up for her, and there she was seated, proudly, receiving the homage of those who, she had once told Harry, had looked the other way when she and Maier had needed someplace to hide after he killed the man; and no refuge had been offered. But it was all forgotten, all forgotten in the years and the champagne, and she was happy now. Bess had been pushed aside almost unnoticed; perhaps Cecilia Weiss had been wrong, this moment was all hers, all hers and her son's. The Great Houdini's mother. It was headstone enough.

Then she felt him release her hand. Ehrich was pushing his way through the relatives to his Catholic American wife, standing forlornly alone near the ornate gold grand piano beside the uniformed string quartet which had been playing Franz Lizst's "Hungarian Rhapsody"—in Budapest, they would have been arrested for playing anything else.

"Are you ready?" he asked Bess.

"Harry, I don't think I can."

Frightened again. He couldn't let it spoil this moment; he had laid everything out so carefully. None of the relatives spoke English, and this was the only way his wife could communicate with them, the only way she could prove she was part of the family.

"I've been teaching you the words for a week! You finally learned the French, didn't you?"

"Harry, please—" She was shaking again.

"They'll have to accept you," he told her. "It's the Jewish 'Star Spangled Banner.' " And before she could protest further, he had given the pianist the signal and the quartet was playing the introduction to "Hatikvah."

And Harry left her there alone.

Slowly, hesitantly, Bess started to sing the strange Hebrew words to the difficult melody. She knew what they meant. Harry had explained them—it was a song expressing a hope that went back centuries. "I am five thousand years old," Cecilia had once told her. This song said it all—next year in Jerusalem, next year, from the Diaspora scattered all over the world, back home. It would be almost half a century more before it would become a reality; but this night, in Budapest, a Gentile singing about their hope was reality enough.

One by one, the relatives turned to stare at her, this foreign *shiksa* with the lovely voice and the terrible Hebrew pronunciation. Some of them started to sing with her. Harry had returned to stand by his mother's side and take her hand. She looked up as his voice joined the others, and saw that he was watching his wife.

Now Bess was singing her heart out. More joined in the song, and more. Until finally it was too much for an old *yenta*.

Mrs. Weiss stood up from her chair, pushed the relatives aside, and rushed to the stairway. She looked over her shoulder to see if her son was following. He was. Good. She stumbled suddenly on the stairs, clutching at her heart, and sank to the steps as Harry ran to her side. The relatives had stopped singing. Harry anxiously massaged his mother's hands and checked her pulse. She opened her eyes for a moment to watch him, then returned to her performance, moaning.

Bess had faltered in the melody. Now she stopped altogether, and watched the tableau on the stairs. They were all crowding around Mrs. Weiss, the center of attention once more. Harry was kissing her hands. Bess felt the anger pulsing at her temples. She knew what she had to do. Drawing herself up with determination, she took a deep breath and started to sing a solo, *a capella* this time—she was undoubtedly the only one in the grand ballroom of the Budapest Royal Hotel who knew the words.

> *"Onward, Christian soldiers,*
> *Marching as to war!"*

She saw Mama's eyes fly open. Mrs. Weiss, at least, understood English. Especially this English.

> *"With the cross of Jesus*
> *Going on before!"*

Cecilia Weiss moaned.

The act was over, the hurt was real.

In all the years that followed, this was one more anguish for which she never forgave them.

## INTERMISSION

HARRY HOUDINI returned to America to become the most famous magician since Moses played his matinee for Pharaoh. Harry's challenges and escapes became legend; his name was in the dictionary, planted there by his personal press agent, who invented the word "Houdinize" and went nameless himself in retribution.

Harry and Bess toured the country, and being noticed was the whole trick. In every city, Harry would head for the largest newspaper and offer to be suspended upside down from its roof, fettered securely in a straitjacket, to free himself for their photographers. Crowds of over 50,000 showed up in the streets to watch. The newspaper could hardly ignore a man hanging by his heels outside their editorial offices, fighting his way out of the shackles of ordinariness.

He was constantly buying illusions from other magicians and making them his own. All over the country, all over the world, he performed his famous Milk Can escape; it became his symbol.

"Houdini's Death Defying Mystery," shouted the billboards. "Escape from a galvanized iron can filled with water and secured by massive locks. Failure Means a Drowning Death!"

In the theater, a large milk can was brought onstage and filled to the brim after a committee from the audience examined it and pronounced it solid. Then Harry, in that ridiculous bathing suit, was handcuffed by a uniformed policeman.

"Ladies and gentlemen!" he would announce, as if they hadn't all been watching. "I have just been handcuffed by a uniformed policeman, and now I'm going to test your ability to hold your breath."

He grabbed a rope, and Franz Kukol and another assistant would help him to drop into the can so forcefully that water cascaded over its sides to the stage. The orchestra would be playing, appropriately, "Anchors Aweigh."

"Ladies and gentlemen!" His head and shoulders were visible above the top of the huge milk can. "On that clock on the side of the stage you will see sixty seconds elapse, second by second. At the moment I submerge myself, take a deep breath and hold it as long as you can. And here I go!"

He would take a deep breath and submerge as Franz poured in more water until the milk can was full to the brim and overflowing, Harry completely underwater. Bess would stand by the clock as it ticked off the seconds. The audience would begin, as a game, holding their breath. By the time thirty seconds had elapsed most of them would have collapsed, gasping, unable to hold on any longer, laughing as they watched their neighbors in the same predicament, and then return their attention to the stage, where Harry Houdini was still underwater. Forty seconds. Fifty. Fifty-five. Sixty. Bess would rap on the side of the can and Harry would shoot up out of the water, _hands_ still manacled, and shout, panting heavily, "And now for the real test!"

He would drop down into the can again, sending the water pouring over its sides. The assistants would again fill it to the brim as the clock started once more to tick off the seconds. Twenty. Thirty. The heavy lid of the milk can was lifted into place now, fastened by six steel bands, each band locked to a steel hasp on the can with padlocks fastened and checked by the committee. The endurance contest was under way.

"Lower the drape," Bess would shout. "Stand by with the fire axes in case of trouble!"

Two assistants in slickers, carrying huge fire axes glinting in the spotlight, would take up their stations as a drape was lowered from the flies.

Ninety seconds. Two minutes. The orchestra increased the tempo of the music. Every member of the audience realized that by this time, if he were inside that milk can, he would be drowning. Two minutes and a half. Two minutes and three-quarters. Three minutes. Still no sign of the Great Houdini. From somewhere in the flies, a stagehand shouted, "Something's gone wrong!" Three minutes and twenty seconds. "He ain't gettin' out!"

Women were leaping to their feet in the audience, calling, "Save him! He's drowning! Get him out!" Three minutes and thirty seconds.

"Take up the drape," shouted Bess frantically. "Take it up!"

"It's stuck," hollered Franz Kukol.

"My God! My God!" Three minutes and fifty seconds. Four minutes. "Get the axes! Get the axes!" Four minutes and ten seconds. The whole audience was screaming now. "Close the curtains!" The curtains were closing, the orchestra stopped playing, the house lights came on, people were running up on stage, panic-stricken, when, suddenly, through the drape appeared the hand of Harry Houdini, clutching at the air. Then he fell out onto the stage from the top of the milk can, which was still firmly padlocked, and collapsed, water pouring off his body, just as the curtains closed about him and Bess rushed to his side to kiss him. Those climbing onto the stage stopped, realizing they had been tricked—those who hadn't been planted in the audience as shouters in the first place—and since that's what they had paid their money for, illusion, they began to applaud. Houdini had done it again, and Harry was on his feet, bowing, one hand holding the manacles above his head, the other clutching Bess, as he smiled, and waved, and triumphed, and the applause rolled over him.

Showbiz. But one day, he would cry "Wolf" too often.

The gimmick that had allowed him to get out of the milk can was a simple one, but it required assistants like Franz Kukol who could substitute milk-can lids at the right moment. The escape from a safe required no gimmicks, but it did require preparation. A safe company would announce its latest monster, weighing many tons, which would defy any attempt of a mere man, even a man like Harry Houdini, to escape from its massive steel. The safe would be brought to the theater and Harry would announce that it was so heavy the stage would have to be reinforced. During the week this was taking place, the safe would remain in the lobby, where it could be examined by anyone. Including Harry, who waited until after midnight when the theater was empty.

Safes are meant to keep burglars out, not to keep anyone in, as Harry well knew. The locking mechanism of any safe must be available, inside the safe, for oiling and checking. All that was necessary was to remove a small plate that covered the tumblers. The springs holding them in position could then be removed, one by one, and weaker springs substituted.

When, with great fanfare, the safe was rolled out on the reinforced stage and Harry was carefully searched and placed inside it, all he had to do was produce a tiny screwdriver and unfasten the plate, then manipulate the weakened tumblers to release the combination. The huge door would swing open at a touch.

But that took only about one minute. The audience must be brought to the same pitch of excitement as by the fear of drowning in a milk can. How much could they take?

Harry had a small camp chair placed at the rear of the safe. After he released himself, he would sit and read a newspaper or magazine as the orchestra played an ominous melody. A half-hour would pass. An hour. Sometimes Bess would slip behind the curtain and whisper to him to stop rustling the pages of the newspaper. The audience could hear.

"Tell the orchestra to play louder," Harry would tell her, if the article were interesting—that is if it were about Harry Houdini—and continue to read. After an hour and a half, by which time the audience was near hysteria, certain Harry had perished from lack of oxygen, he would remove his jacket and tie, tear his shirt, throw a glass of water over his forehead to simulate perspiration, and stagger through the curtain, almost collapsing with exhaustion, to collect his applause and his weekly check.

Another of his most successful illusions was that of walking through a brick wall, built by four bricklayers onstage in full view of the audience. It was this illusion that caused Sir Arthur Conan Doyle to swear he had felt Houdini dematerialize his body before passing through it. Harry shrugged. It was all right with him, as long as that check materialized on schedule.

Harry escaped from a coffin, from a packing case hurled into New York Harbor from a tugboat, from a straitjacket twenty stories above Times Square. He became the first man to fly in Australia, of all places, because flying was dangerous and people expected it of him.

By the time he made a full-sized elephant vanish from the block-long stage of the New York Hippodrome, Harry Houdini had become the highest-paid performer in the history of vaudeville. On that day, he hurried with Bess to their brownstone home on 113th Street, the lavish residence he had once announced was the most expensive house ever purchased by a magician. It had cost him the unheard-of sum of $25,000, proving that economics makes its own magic.

Harry had changed his entire week's salary into gold coins at the bank, and now he poured them into Mama's apron, as he had promised her all those light-years ago.

The effect was not what he had intended. Cecilia had been ill. She was seated on the couch in the luxurious living room, a nurse in attendance. Her son Theo was also a visitor that night.

She held the gold coins in her apron, and the tears started.

"Mama! What is it this time?"

"Money I don't want. I'm a sick woman. What I want is my son should stay home, not run off to Europe again, I might never see him." She clutched at her heart pathetically.

"The doctor said you'll be all right," Bess told her, worried that the whole performance was about to begin again.

"So what do doctors know?"

Harry dropped to his knees beside the couch.

"Mama, I have to fill the engagements, I have contracts. Theo will be here, and Nate, and Leo, everybody, you've got a maid, a nurse. You think for a minute I'd leave if the doctor had said there was any danger?"

"*You* talked to the doctor, or the Catholic talked?"

Since that night in Budapest, the Holy War had continued.

"You think she'd lie about a thing like that?"

Cecilia Weiss didn't answer. She didn't have to.

"Mama, listen to me. I think it's about time you stopped acting like a child, I think it's time you said you forgive!"

The old temper flared.

"When I'm dead and buried, I'll forgive!" And she brushed the coins off her lap onto the floor. "Go, pick up your gold, Ehrich, that's all your *shiksa* wants!"

## ACT SIX

THE cable arrived at the theater in Hamburg, but Harry and Bess had already left to play an engagement in Copenhagen. It took several days for it to catch up with them. When the message that his mother had suffered a stroke and was not expected to live was handed to Harry before a performance, he turned around and went back to his hotel. For the first time in his life, Harry Houdini missed a performance. He was incapable of functioning. Bess had to make the arrangements to get back to America, had to pack his clothes for him, had to get him out of the city. He could barely speak, consumed with grief, consumed with guilt.

Breaching a contract is a criminal offense in Denmark, and the police arrested Franz Kukol, thinking he was Harry. Franz had to spend a fearful night in jail until the situation was explained. The theater manager withdrew his charges.

Harry and Bess managed to catch the same ocean liner for the return trip on which they had sailed from America. But before they could board it, word came that Cecilia Weiss was dead.

Machpelach Cemetery was not so crowded all those years ago. There was room between the stones for the guests yet to come. Bess walked anxiously down the pathway, knowing full well what she would find. After all these months, Harry still spent two hours a day at his mother's grave.

She saw him now, on his knees, his face in his hands, before the stone. A pile of pebbles told their story. He came here to talk to Mama, he actually spoke aloud, they had all heard him, the rest of the family, when they came occasionally to mourn. Harry barely bothered to shave any more; he had given up the act, over Bess's remonstrances, and had lost interest in a magic that had no power to bring his mother back.

She crossed quietly to his side. That coat he's wearing, she thought, that has to be thrown out. And that terrible hat. He looks like an immigrant. One more week without shaving, he'll look just like his father, the rabbi.

"Harry?" She said it gently. He didn't look up. She knelt beside him.

"Harry, for God's sake. It's almost a year now. Your mother's dead."

Now he raised his head. His face was haggard, his eyes red.

"Why did they bury her before we got back?"

"She was in New York, we were in Copenhagen. Do I have to draw a diagram?"

"I should never have left. It's my fault, all my fault."

"It's mine, if it's anyone's. I insisted we keep the bookings."

"She was trying to tell me something before she died. She called my name."

"Theo was with her, and he says he couldn't hear, she was so weak."

"If only she was saying she forgave me, maybe I could rest, maybe I could sleep."

He let Bess help him to his feet. She led him toward a bench.

"Harry, stop torturing yourself. It isn't going to bring her back."

She sat beside him.

"Hammerstein's been calling. He wants you again at the Victoria, more money than ever, six weeks firm. Think of all the fun you could have. Jump off a few more bridges. Hang in a straitjacket. Enjoy."

"Tell him to talk to Theo. I'm giving Theo the act; I don't want it any more, ever."

His tone made her think of Mama, fainting on

the stairway in the grand ballroom, but still with presence of mind to look around and see how she was going over. The Great Houdini was drowning before her eyes in a milk can of self-pity. Someone ought to play "Anchors Aweigh."

Bess stood up.

"What do you want?" she asked him. "To come here every day for another ten months, feeling sorry? To stop eating, stop living, turn yourself into a wreck? You haven't gone to bed with me since Copenhagen. I'm not dead yet."

He put his arms around her.

"Bess . . . Bess . . ."

"Don't you think I know?" She was stroking his hair. Strange how she had grown up during their marriage and he had not. "I feel empty, too. Who will I have to hate?"

She lifted his chin with her hand, so she could see his face.

"That was supposed to make you smile," Bess said. "I'm as sorry for her as you are. But I'm trying to be sensible while you . . . Come on, Harry, be a *mensch*. You'll have a breakdown."

She thought she was getting through to him.

"You don't understand," he said. "Mama's gone."

Bess pushed him away from her.

"Goddammit, I *do* understand! It's not natural, Harry. This isn't you." She had felt it, she had felt something strange, when she had entered the cemetery. We all do, in the presence of the legions of the dead. But this feeling had been different.

Bess turned and pointed at the grave.

"The old *yenta*'s trying to pull you in there. She always wanted you to sleep with *her*."

If she had wanted to rouse him, she had succeeded. Harry leaped from the bench and grabbed her fiercely, eyes glaring at her.

"Don't you dare talk about Mama like that! She's dead!" And he shook her, and Bess fell, slipping out of his grasp, fell to the damp grass of the cold cemetery, in front of Mama's headstone, the one Harry had paid for.

Slowly, she got to her feet.

"I've done all I can for you, Harry," she said, "but I can't fight a ghost. I'm leaving you. I should have done it long ago. Maybe you'll come to your senses."

She turned away and started down the walk. Harry followed, not ready to believe her.

"How can you talk about leaving me when I'm so upset?"

She stopped.

"You want me to wait until you're happy?"

"All right, go!" he shouted.

"I'm going, I'm going!" she shouted back.

That was their relationship now. To communicate, they shouted.

Harry was following her again.

"Why?" he wanted to know. "Why are you doing this to me?"

He honestly doesn't know, she thought. So she turned to face him again.

"Harry," she said, in control of herself now, "when was the last time you told me you loved me? For that matter, when was the first time?"

Her husband looked puzzled.

"What the hell's that got to do with it?"

"When was the last time you told your mother?"

"She was an old lady, what do you want?"

"Queen Victoria's dress, that's what I want."

And she left him, standing among the graves.

"**¡SABNBRANS YNAMABÐ**" read the newsreel title, inverted because Harry was backstage at the Victoria behind the movie screen with Theo, who looked uncomfortable in the traditional tuxedo of the stage magician as he helped the attendants arrange the props for the act, which was now called "Hardeen, the Magnificent." The Magnificent had one arm in a sling. The newsreel was continuing, the events of World War I leading up to the surrender of the Kaiser's armies fitfully illuminating their faces.

"I almost drowned in your milk can," Theo was accusing his brother. It was Harry's fault Theo was five inches taller and had difficulty getting into any of Harry's props. "Last week I dislocated my shoulder in your straitjacket." He indicated the sling. "Somebody put a pair of handcuffs on me, took me three hours to escape, the whole audience went home. How much do I have to pay you to take the act back?" He pointed to the movie screen. "They fought a whole war, you were crying in a cemetery, trying to starve yourself to death."

"Will you come with me after the show? To Boston?"

Theo stared at his *meshugeneh* brother.

"So what's in Boston after midnight?"

"Someone who can help us. They say she can let me talk to Mama."

"Five minutes to curtain, Theo." He turned.

Daisy White was approaching them, the same Daisy, younger, softer, the form-fitting tights and low-cut blouse of a magician's assistant giving an accent to her sexuality that was hardly necessary. You could have dressed Daisy White as a Mother Superior and the Pope would have had to go to confession.

"Five minutes to curtain," she repeated.

"Daisy, the Great Houdini's gone crazy, you worry about a curtain?"

Daisy turned to look at Harry, dirty, unshaven Harry, and her eyes widened.

"*You're* Mr. Houdini?"

"He changed himself into a bum," Theo explained. "It's one of his most amazing tricks."

"When I was a kid," Daisy told Harry, almost in awe, "I saw you dive off a bridge, handcuffed. I thought you were gonna kill yourself."

"So did I," Harry said, turning back to his

brother. She was a magician's assistant, that's all.
They were all cut from the same seductive mold;
it was part of the business. "I'm not crazy. This
medium's been investigated, and some of the greatest scientists say it's true. All I want to find out
is what Mama was trying to tell me. Did she forgive? Did she?"

"Harry—"

"I got a letter from Conan Doyle, in England,
he swears this woman let him speak to his son, the
son that was killed in the war."

"Harry, look." Theo pointed to the movie screen.
The film was panning the endless rows of crosses
in an Allied cemetery in France. "After every war,
so many dead, every father, every mother, hopes
one, one of all the millions, can get through, and
you know? Not one. Never, Harry. But the mediums
make a fortune. Mama never called collect."

He turned away, the matter finished, to prepare
for the ordeal that was his magic act. Harry grabbed
him by the shoulder—the bad one. Theo winced.

"Theo, who knows what's impossible? This
woman in Boston is different, there's scientific
proof of—"

"Scientific proof! For God's sake, Harry, you of
all people! Don't be a sucker!"

"Don't worry. She wouldn't dare try to trick
*me*."

"You're right. Not Harry Houdini, she wouldn't
try. But who are you today? A wreck; a shaking

nervous wreck. A bum. Remember, your own brother told you. Don't try to talk to Mama. Why don't you talk to Bess, for God's sake?"

"I'm never talking to Bess."

"All right. But don't go to some cockamamie midnight mass, don't believe in miracles, Harry."

The orchestra struck up the overture, Harry's overture. Theo picked up his top hat and set it on his head. It didn't fit too well.

"Excuse me," he said, "I gotta go walk through a brick wall. I hope I make it."

He started for the center of the stage.

Harry stood there, miserably alone. Daisy hadn't taken her eyes off him. Now she crossed, and put her hand on his.

"Believe in miracles," she said. "What else is there?"

# ACT SEVEN

MINA CRANDON was to become the most famous medium of the golden age of Spiritualism. She was an extremely attractive and vivacious woman, blue-eyed and blond-haired, with a lovely figure she took little pains to hide. She was the third wife of a prominent Boston surgeon who was on the faculty of Harvard Medical School. They lived at Number 10 Lime Street, Boston, an address that was soon to become famous.

When the stories of the strange psychic phenomena that occurred in her home started to circulate, her real name was kept secret to protect her position in Boston society. The phenomena became so startling that *Scientific American*, the solid journal of American scientific thought, sent one of its investigators to observe her seances. His name was Malcolm Bird, and he authenticated absolutely all the weird miracles that were happening, concealing her true identity by referring to her as "Margery," a name that became known throughout the world.

Many of the strange happenings in her darkened seance room came from ectoplasm. According to spiritualist belief, ectoplasm is the material from which the spirits draw their energy. If the power is strong enough, the ectoplasm allows the spirit to materialize from it. Should white light strike it, it withdraws within the body of the medium, often with disastrous results. Consequently all white light is barred from serious seances. Ectoplasm, the articles in *Scientific American* stated, issued during seances from Margery's mouth, nose, navel, and vagina. It usually assumed the shape of crude hands, misshapen, but recognizable because of five clawlike projections from the main mass.

Startled by the documentation of such a strange revelation, the Dingwall Society for Psychical Research in London, one of the most respected of the time, subjected Margery to a scientific investigation of its own, a seance in England, using red light for observation. After the manifestation, they reported they saw a "long, thin, tonguelike structure issuing, not in motion but apparently arrested in its development, from a slit in Margery's robe, beneath which she wore no clothing. While the medium was apparently in a deep trance, the red light showed a hideous, limp and flaccid hand protruding from Margery's exposed vagina and connected to the unbilical opening."

Further, the medium spoke during her trance with the voice of her dead brother, Walter, who had died twenty years earlier in a train wreck. He was a coarse and vulgar individual whose conversation consisted of four-letter words. Certainly, no lady of the time could have known, or dared pronounce, such language. The voice issuing from Margery obviously had to be coming from another world.

Harry had heard all of this, and discounted most of it. But in his depression he was clutching at straws. And Sir Arthur Conan Doyle had attested to her ability to contact the dead.

Dr. Le Roi Crandon introduced Harry to his miraculous wife as they stood in the luxuriously furnished study of his Boston home, illuminated only by candles arranged in the form of a crucifix. In that light, Margery was startlingly beautiful, almost virginal, in appearance. She wore a diaphanous dressing down and slippers, and took Harry's hand in her own.

"I hope so desperately I can help you." Her voice was low, gentle, sincere.

"I'm more desperate than you are," Harry said. He was still distraught, but he had shaved, he had fortified himself with six cups of coffee, he had prepared as carefully as he could for this meeting.

He wanted to believe, but on his own terms. He was still Harry Houdini.

"If Mama could really . . ." He hesitated. "Look, I'm a professional magician. All my life I work with tricks, sleight-of-hand." How could he say it without offending her? "What I'm trying to say is, I have to be sure *you* don't."

"I have no tricks hidden under this robe, I assure you. I have nothing at all." She smiled at him. "Will you take my word for it?"

Not the Great Houdini.

"I'm from New York," he said, "but pretend I'm from Missouri."

"With the greatest pleasure," said Margery, and opened the robe wide.

Harry looked, and nodded.

"Nice," he said.

"No, Mr. Houdini. Sensational."

He had to agree. Her perfectly formed breasts, her hips, her vagina—he remembered the reports, could they be true?—stirred him, and he remembered how long it had been since he had been a man. Much too long. But this was no time for that. A bum, his brother had called him, a shaking nervous wreck.

"I've been stripped naked and still had things hidden on me," Harry said. He remembered the rumor. Her husband, the surgeon, had performed a strange hysterectomy, leaving her a hiding place no one would suspect.

Dr. Crandon was watching him.

"You have my permission to conduct a thorough search of the premises," he said, urbanely, a little amused.

Harry looked at Margery. Would she? She stepped closer to him.

"I insist." She opened the robe wider. Harry dropped to his knees to investigate the sensuous body.

"I'm going to make a believer of you tonight, Mr. Houdini," Margery told him.

"Well, I'll say this," Harry said, and there was no denying the tremor in his voice, "if you can't raise the dead, nobody can."

Margery laughed.

"Don't worry," she said, "I can."

In the darkness she cried out, "Walter! Walter . . . are you there? Answer me . . . this is Margery."

Harry held her left hand firmly in his, his foot pressed on her slipper. Dr. Crandon held her other hand. There were two other couples in the eerie room, dark except for the distant glow of the candles. Harry could feel the sexuality of the moment. It was always male and female in a darkened room, touching; hadn't he said the same thing to Bess in the dim past? "Death is the only enemy; we have to show him life is stronger." The Spiritualists knew. It was an expression of life-giving sex, you could almost scent it in the air, along with the

fear and the wonder that accentuated it, the touch
of the beautiful medium at his side, that made it
easier to believe anything, that the boundaries had
been pushed aside and that the unknown could be
within that darkened room.

"Walter? Walter? Where are you?"

An eerie whistling filled the room. It seemed to
be coming from everywhere and nowhere, faintly,
then stronger. It was the melody of Drdla's
"Souvenir." Harry had been told it was Walter's
favorite song.

"Walter?"

"Goddammit, Margery, I was busy, what the fuck
do you want?"

Harry was startled. The voice was rough, hoarse,
baritone. It seemed to be coming from Margery's
body, but that was impossible.

"We have an unbeliever here tonight," she said,
and her voice was dreamlike; she had fallen into
a trance as the lights had been lowered. "Give us
a sign that you are here."

A dinner bell rang in the darkness, a tambourine
sounded and then rolled out onto the floor from
beneath the table. Both objects had been placed
there earlier, out of the medium's reach.

"Parlor tricks," Harry said. This kind of trickery
he understood.

"Shut your godddam mouth." Walter's voice
sounded annoyed, impatient. He wasn't used to
being doubted.

"Forgive him, Walter." Margery was sad, sympathetic. "He is in desperate grief. His mother passed over."

"Yes, I know," Walter said impatiently. "She's here now. Mama is here."

And as he said it, the ectoplasm appeared, in the shape of a hand, eerily visible in the dim light, the hand moving above the table, moving toward Harry, slowly, strangely.

"She's searching for him now," Walter said.

"We see her hand," Margery assured him. "It is moving toward us . . ."

A face appeared in the darkness, above the table, above the hand, the face of an old woman, floating, disembodied.

"Harry . . . Harry . . ." The voice was old, tired, distant, ghostly, calling to him pitifully. "Harry, where are you? Answer me, my son."

"Mama, speak Yiddish so I'll know it's you." Harry's voice was mocking. "*Rade Yiddish, du herst?*"

There was a strained silence. Yiddish was a strange language to be heard in Boston. The eerie face seemed frozen momentarily. Then, again, the ghostly voice: "It is not spoken in Heaven, my son."

"Then get the hell outta there, Mama," shouted Harry. "Heaven is restricted!" And simultaneously he leaped to his feet, the railroad flare he had concealed in his jacket now in his hand, bursting into brilliant red flame as he pulled the igniter. Everyone was shrieking and shouting. In the glare and the smoke, Margery could be seen, standing stark naked on her chair, holding a pair of tongs to which were attached the luminous face. The hand that Harry had been holding during the seance was of rubber, filled with warm water, attached inside the sleeve of the robe she had discarded. Her foot had been slipped out of her slipper; her husband had released her on the other side.

She was shrieking in rage at the top of her voice, her nude body reflecting the revealing flame.

"You lying whore!" Harry was shouting at her, almost sobbing, "You dirty bitch!"

"YOU'RE GOING TO DIE!" The voice was Walter's but the words came from Margery's lovely lips. "I'LL SEE YOU DEAD AND GONE, YOU BASTARD!"

The music box was playing "Rosabelle" in the darkness. Harry stood beside the mantel and listened, just listened, for a while. Then he lit a match. His hand trembled as he lit the *Yortzeit* candle under his mother's picture. A year. A whole year since she had left him. He thought he heard the doorbell ringing, but he disregarded it. The shock of the meeting with Mina Crandon had taken too much out of him. If only he could die, he thought, maybe that was the only way, go to them, cross the line to *them*, don't expect the dead to come to you, why should they bother to make such a difficult journey when it was so easy for you to go the other way? You wouldn't take a little trip to see your own mother?

The doorbell again. Mechanically, he closed the music box and crossed to the front door, his slippers slapping on his bare feet, the bathrobe a little threadbare without a wife to see it got mended. When he opened the door he was startled to see that it was bright daylight outside. He had kept the curtains closed in the house for so long he had lost track of time. There was a girl standing on the doorstep. It was Bess, looking exactly as she did when they first met. His heart leaped—she had come, she had made the first move. Why did she look so young? Had he gone back in time, so Mama was still alive and Bess was still young? How wonderful!

"Bess!" He reached for her. "Where have you been?"

"It's Daisy White, Mr. Houdini." Daisy slipped past his grasp, into the living room, as he turned, trying to wrench himself back to the present. She was wearing a light print dress, and her hair was up. No wonder she looked like Bess; she was young, she was alive, and most important, she had come to him.

"Theo sent me over to see if you've had anything to eat today . . . or this week." She crossed to the tightly closed drapes. "My God, this place is like a morgue."

She swept the drapes open and sunlight flooded into the room, revealing the dirty clothes thrown about, the remnants of the food he had tried to get himself to eat scattered on plates on the couch, the piano.

"I'm all alone," Harry said pleadingly. "You know what that means?" No, he decided, she couldn't know, all alone with your mind, a mind that was slipping away. How could someone like Daisy imagine it, and the fright that went with it?

"You're a mess. Let's go upstairs, we'll get you washed up." She was leading him up the stairs, and her body brushed his. He had almost forgotten.

"You smell lovely," he said.

"Compared to you, a mule would smell lovely."

Daisy steered him upstairs to the bedroom and then into the bath, the one with the oversized tub that he had ordered so he could submerge and practice holding his breath, or fill with ice to help condition the body that he now seemed determined to destroy.

"Get in there and shave," Daisy insisted. "Theo's coming by later to take you to dinner. Don't let him see you like this." She started to remove the old bathrobe, unbuttoning the pajamas, what buttons were left.

"Has he heard from Bess?"

Daisy paused. "I'm not supposed to tell you. Yes. Every day. To find out how you are."

She picked up the straight razor from the sink,

opened it, and placed it in his hand. He stared at
it for a moment, then raised it slowly and held it
in front of him.

"You trust me with this?"

She recognized the gesture. Harry was striking
a pose for her benefit. Macbeth. Is this a dagger
which I see before me? There was always the danger, though, that it would become reality. She felt
a sorrow for him—he used to dive off bridges,
now you couldn't trust him in the bathroom. His
helplessness touched her. She had never thought
of the Great Houdini as needing anyone, herself
least of all.

"Mr. Houdini, I got nobody in this whole goddam world," she heard herself saying. "My boy
friend left me, I had an abortion, I don't have a
nickel in the bank, but *I* still wanna live. And I'm
stupid. Go ahead, shave."

She turned to start out.

"Daisy, don't leave me alone!"

She knew then. It was the hopelessness in his
voice. She would. But she never intended to fall in
love with him.

"I'm here," she said. "I'm not leaving. I wouldn't
leave now no matter what."

And she walked into the bedroom, slowly.

"Thank you," Harry said. He ran the water into
the basin. He picked up the shaving soap and the
brush. But he discovered he'd forgotten what to
do next.

"I must have seen your picture in the papers a hundred times." Daisy's voice, Daisy was around somewhere, he couldn't see her. "Jumping off a bridge, breaking out of jail, getting buried in a coffin. You always got out. I felt like you were doing it for me. 'See, Daisy? There's always hope!' "

He shook his head.

"Bullshit. There's no hope. Not for me. Right now I'd like to die."

"Oh, no you wouldn't."

Something in her voice made him look up. There, in the mirror, he saw her, in his bed, sitting up nakedly unashamed, her clothes scattered nearby. She held out her arms, offering the only thing she had of value, to help him, to comfort him.

"Come to bed, Harry," she called.

Harry stared. This was the moment he had waited for for so long. He started toward her. She was with him again. She was there.

"All right, Mama," he said.

## ACT EIGHT

"WE have to keep it out of the papers," Theo told Bess on the telephone. "The doctor sent him to Bellevue."

"Can I see him?" The papers, what the hell did the papers matter any more?

"Do you want to?"

"Theo, don't be as stupid as your brother. I'm going down to get him out of there."

"The doctor said—"

"I don't give a damn."

"The doctor says it's acute melancholia, he has to—"

"Doctors have a good name for everything they don't understand. He'll die in there. I'm going to get him out if I have to blow up the hospital."

"Bess." How could he say it? "He didn't ask for you."

"Oh, Theo, don't be a *shlemiehl*. If I'd waited for him to ask first, we'd never have gotten married."

She thought she looked good. She had taken special care with her makeup, something she hadn't bothered about while they were living apart. She had fixed her hair herself; there wasn't time to go to a beauty parlor. She had sworn she would never do it, she would never be the first to give in. Now here she was, in the hospital walking down the corridor of the mental ward where they had shipped him. You could tell it was the mental ward because the rooms had peep holes so the patients could be watched. There was nothing sharp in the rooms, no curtains, nothing they could tie around their necks. There was even a little grille hidden in the wall, from which a guard's eyes kept watch on the corridor.

The windows had bars. Like Scotland Yard.

A nice place to visit, you wouldn't want to live there.

The nurse at her side was Minnie, the Minnie who was to become so important in their lives. Right now she was fearful.

"I'm not even supposed to let you in the room," she told Bess, "but I used to be in show business myself. Chester and Holt. Ever hear of us?"

"I'm sorry, no."

"That's why I'm here. Holt is driving a garbage truck."

Minnie stopped at the nurse's station to pick up his chart. Bess paused and looked through the peep hole into the room. Harry was sitting up in a rocking chair, by the window, silent, unseeing. Whistler's Mother, Bess thought. I'll bet he picked that pose carefully. Gets you right here.

Maybe that was unfair. Maybe Harry wasn't standing back, admiring his own performance. Maybe.

"You think it's all right for me to go in?" she asked Minnie.

The nurse indicated the chart. "There's nothing wrong with him. Except he's getting worse all the time. You figure it out."

Bess had noticed the framed picture of Mama on the table beside Harry.

"She's winning," she said, and followed Minnie into his room.

Harry didn't even turn at their entrance.

"Hello, Harry."

No answer.

"I just happened to be passing by. It's such a nice day, I thought you might want to try a hospital escape."

He hated bad jokes. But he didn't react to this one.

"Harry. Hello."

Nothing.

"Goddammit!" Bess grabbed Mama's picture off the table, smashing it against the bed post as Minnie gasped in surprise and Harry leaped right out of his rocking chair.

"Mrs. Houdini! This is a hospital!"

Harry yanked the shattered photograph from her hands.

"What the hell are you doing, Bess?"

"Oh, *now* he recognizes me."

He turned away.

"Hello," she said.

"Where you been?" He finally acknowledged her presence.

"Right here. Right here all the goddam time. All you had to do was crook your finger. You never bothered."

"You're the one who walked out."

"You're the one who made me."

"Score tied, one all," Minnie said.

"Get out, you old bag."

"He's normal," Minnie told Bess. "I'll be right outside if he gets violent." And she left.

Harry turned to Bess. "I'm sorry, I'm sorry. I didn't want you to know how much I missed you."

She held back the tears, the anger almost more than she could bear.

"Where's *my* picture, Harry?" she asked quietly.

He turned away.

"Goddammit, why did you come here if you're

going to start that again?"

"To get you loose from the apron strings that are pulling you into the grave!"

She tried to grab the picture back, but he held on.

"Bess!" It was all right, she felt, it was going to be all right, he was fighting her again. She picked the card off the little bouquet of roses; she had seen it instantly when she walked into the room.

"Who's Daisy?" she inquired, innocently, reading the card.

"A girl, works in Theo's act. I hardly know her."

"Liar."

He looked at her. Telepathy he didn't believe in. Woman's intuition, maybe.

"How do you know?"

"I sent her to you."

Harry sat down again.

"Jesus Christ! The hell you did."

"The truth, Harry, the *emiss*, I'm not out of my mind, I just told her to find out how you were, to cheer you up. I didn't expect her to cheer you up right into the hospital." She shrugged. "She's sick, too, how did I know?"

"How could you have come here, knowing that?"

"I can fight her, she's alive. And I love you, and she has no idea what that is. But your mother's putting up a tougher fight than I expected."

Harry got to his feet.

"I tried to talk to Mama, did you know that? I went to a seance." He turned, he smiled at the thought. "Would you believe, *I* went to a seance?"

"It was all over the papers."

"I haven't seen a newspaper in months."

"Margery said Mama appeared in the room and you were crying and calling her name, over and over."

"That bitch! That phony bitch! There isn't one lousy trick she does I couldn't do ten times better! Somebody ought to drive those grave robbers out of business."

He was pacing now.

"Go ahead," Bess said.

"How, go ahead?"

"Make it part of the act."

He stopped pacing.

"We still got an act?"

"You tell me."

"How?"

"You know damn well how.".

"The dress is gone."

"Not the dress, it never really was the dress." She crossed to him and indicated the shattered photograph he was still holding in his hands. She was hoping the tears wouldn't come. "Tell her you love me the best, I want her to hear."

There was a silence.

"Look at your wedding ring," Harry said. "It's engraved."

"That's not enough."

"It was all I had." Couldn't she understand?

"My whole act!" He put his arms around her. "So I don't ever have to say it. Just believe me. Until I die. No, even after I die. Believe." He looked down at her. "My God, she's crying again."

"You all right, Harry?" she wanted to know, fighting to control her voice. "You really all right? Your blood pressure and everything?"

"Physically, the doctor says I'm fine."

She looked up at him.

"Then please, Harry," she said. "Please."

There was no mistaking her meaning. He looked around. Then he picked her up in his arms and almost threw her onto the bed. He reached over and pulled the screen in front of them, so no one could see through the peep hole.

She was sighing in his arms when the door opened suddenly, revealing Minnie and a doctor, clinical in his white coat. Minnie took one startled glance at the bed and shoved him back into the corridor.

"Never mind, doctor," she said hastily. "Someone else is taking his temperature."

## ACT NINE

AS with everything Harry did, he threw himself into his exposé of spiritualism with every resource at his command. The act went back on the boards with a new dimension, a controversy that over the years built into national proportions. Harry published a pamphlet, "Houdini Exposes the Tricks Used by the Boston Medium 'Margery,' " that caused a storm of protest from her admirers. He hired women as investigators to get evidence for him to present onstage when the mediums or their followers appeared in his audiences at the theater and challenged him. Some of his investigators told of being taken into dark rooms by ministers of the Spiritualist religion who would tell them solemnly their dead husbands wanted them to have sexual relations with the minister so they could communicate better.

Harry started visiting the mediums himself, sometimes in the disguise of an old man in a wheel chair. At a crucial moment during a seance he would leap out of the chair, pull off his wig, and introduce his companions—usually reporters from the local newspapers. Bess thought he was enjoying his impersonations more than the act; she accused him of taking bows in front of ghosts, but he laughed her off and continued his exposés throughout the United States and on their tours of Europe.

Harry even took a plunge into motion pictures, daring the greatest Unknown of all, and found out that not even Harry Houdini could escape from the Bank of America. He made a sensational series of four consecutive flops starring himself, and lost most of the money he and Bess had saved up over the years. On film, he played a hero who performed all of Houdini's great escapes in order to outwit the villains. But he had forgotten the one ingredient that had made his stage appearances successful: no audience knew when they walked into a vaudeville theater whether they were going to see Houdini finally kill himself. In a motion picture, the suspense was gone. Harry only died at the box office.

So it was back to the vaudeville he loved, and the continuation of his drive against the Spiritualists, which had become the single-minded aim of his life. Harry was showman enough to know it wasn't sufficient to bring his public back. He introduced a new escape that became a sensation, the Chinese Water Torture, billing it modestly as "Houdini's own original invention, the greatest sensational mystery ever attempted in this or any other age." It developed from the Milk Can stunt, which had one basic flaw: the audience could never see that he was actually under water inside it. The Water Torture was a huge, iron-bound tank, one side of it glass. Harry's feet would be imprisoned in stocks and padlocked; he would then be hauled up, upside down, and lowered into the huge tank until he was visible behind the glass under five feet of water. The stocks were then padlocked to the top of the tank and checked by a committee. A curtain was pulled up around the tank, the pit orchestra wound the audience up to fever pitch, and at the last possible moment, Harry would leap out from behind the curtains, exhausted but free as the drapes around the tank dropped to reveal it was still filled with water, the padlocks still solidly in place. It was a punishing escape, requiring tremendous breath control and athletic ability, but it brought audiences to their feet, and Harry performed it, night after night. The applause made it all worth while.

But the spirit exposés were still the heart of his performance. In city after city, he methodically exposed the mediums, some of whom had developed fanatic followings at a time when the Spiritualist movement was growing to tremendous proportions. Members of the Spiritualist Church filed criminal libel suits against him, totaling over a million dollars, but Harry continued, not only in the act, but in a series of lectures at colleges and universities.

Threats were being made against him now; more than one medium openly predicted his untimely death. The spirits, they said, had been aroused, manifestations were being received from the Other World, it was a time of danger and mystery, tremendous forces wanted his life.

And then Harry Houdini was subpoenaed to appear before a subcommittee of the Sixty-ninth Congress in Washington, D.C., where he and Bess were concluding a stage engagement. He had become a national issue.

He was to testify concerning an ordinance banning fortunetellers from the District of Columbia; the bill, introduced by Representative Sol Bloom of New York, was broad enough to force Washington's mediums out of business. If it succeeded, the future of the Spiritualist Church in America was threatened.

The night before the hearing, backstage at the Washington Theater, Bess tried to talk Harry out of jeopardizing his career, and possibly his life. The audience that night had been strange, threatening, antagonistic. Washington newspapers had headlines about the controversy, about Harry's scheduled appearance, about the warnings he had received.

"You should never have accused the President of holding seances right in the White House," Bess told him, wiping the makeup off her face; she wore plenty of makeup now, for the years had begun to take their toll, although she was still an attractive woman. Attractive, but frightened again.

"It's the truth," Harry said, as if that were a defense.

"Coolidge believes he can talk to the dead?"

"Don't knock it," said Minnie, who was hanging up the costumes, by now a member of their theatrical family. "It's the first time he's talked since he was elected."

Harry was checking out the Water Torture tank before having it shipped to their next engagement in Detroit. The secret of his miraculous escapes was the hard work that went into seeing that they didn't have to be miraculous.

"Congress just wants my opinion," he insisted.

"But you'll turn it into the Civil War." Minnie had been with him long enough now to understand him better than the doctors in the hospital ever could.

Bess put down her newspaper.

"Those politicians will use it as an excuse to hound you out of the business," she said. "Every God-fearing churchgoer in the country is turning against you, and they all vote."

"Come on, Bess," Harry said. "You were the one who told me to expose the phonies, put it in the act."

"It was a bad idea. I have had bad ideas sometimes."

"Well, I've got a good idea." He was wiping his hands now, having finished inspecting the tank. "Get the act back to where it used to be. I'm going to put the Water Torture at the top of the show."

Bess had never cared for that escape. She knew, and Harry knew, the things that could go wrong with it, if his body was not supple enough to turn around under water in its tiny space.

"Harry, that was all right when you were younger. It's too dangerous for you now."

"What do you want, ring-around-the-rosie? Even those who hate me will buy tickets to see me get killed."

Bess shuddered.

"Don't talk about that. First Margery, then those letters to the newspapers, then that woman in the audience tonight, screaming she had a vision you were going to die next week in Detroit."

"Those hysterical fakes. Wait till I get finished with them at the hearing tomorrow."

He seated himself on a chaise and picked up a newspaper. Bess crossed and sat beside him.

"Don't, Harry. Please."

"Don't what?"

"Anything. If one gimmick goes wrong in that tank, you could drown. Don't testify in Congress. The hearing room will be full of all those nuts, fanatics. They hate you so much, no telling what they'll try." She saw he still took it as a joke. Maybe it was. But why tempt fate? For all Harry's disdain for the supernatural, he still used extra care on Friday the 13th, and he had once walked completely around the block rather than cross the path of a black cat.

She took the newspaper out of his hands to make him look at her.

"Why don't we cancel next week in Detroit? Go away someplace, just the two of us, anyplace we don't find ourselves always talking about death? I got the shivers."

He grinned at her and reached over to kiss her.

There was a knock at the door. Bess whirled.

"Don't let anyone in you don't know, Minnie," she said.

Minnie nodded and crossed to the door of the dressing room. She opened it a crack and peered out. There was a well-dressed couple standing outside, a couple she had never seen before.

"Sir Arthur Conan Doyle," said the man, who had a strange, angular face and a vaudeville mustache, "with Lady Conan Doyle."

"Oh, come on," said Minnie, closing the door in his face and turning away. Probably harmless, but why take a chance?

"Who was it, Minnie?" called Bess.

"Some nut, says he's Sir Somebody with Lady Somebody."

Harry leaped to his feet and crossed to the door, throwing it open just in time to see them turning away.

"Sir Arthur! Lady Conan Doyle! Come in, come in!"

They turned, hesitantly, and started into the dressing room.

"We don't seem to be very welcome," Conan Doyle said. Over the years, he and Harry had remained friendly, but recent events had strained the bonds, and he had thought, reasonably, that perhaps he had made a mistake in coming backstage.

"That's just Minnie's way," Harry assured them, putting his arms about them. "She used to be a bouncer in a house of ill repute."

Minnie sniffed.

"I was never that fortunate," she said. Vaudeville had trained both of them in one-liners. It took the place of conversation.

Bess had crossed to embrace Lady Conan Doyle, an old friend now, so British, so reserved, but so good-hearted. She always wore the height of fashion. That is, it had been the height of fashion when Victoria was alive.

"Jean, so good to see *you!*" Bess said, and she meant it. Lady Conan Doyle was what she was without pretense, so different from some of their show-business friends. "Why didn't you tell us you were in Washington? Were you in the audience tonight?"

"Yes, dear, and I must say we were shocked." Her tone was hurt, distant. Obviously, she had been terribly disturbed by what she had heard in the theater that night.

"You know I'm here to lecture on Spiritualism," Conan Doyle said. The whole world knew he had given up literary work to devote his life to a cause Harry was attempting to destroy. Their friendship had barely survived. "I did resent all of us being called charlatans."

Harry laughed.

"Arthur, I know you're sincere, but most of the others—"

"Harry, we came backstage tonight only because we're frightened for you. Your mother is trying desperately to get in touch with you from the Beyond. She has a warning."

"Bullshit," Harry told him, laughing since they were friends and could say things like that to each other. "Which phony told you that?"

"*This* phony." It was Lady Conan Doyle, angry, hurt, sincere. Harry had heard that she had discovered she was a sensitive, that she practiced automatic writing. She crossed and put her hand on his arm.

"You're in terrible danger," she told him. "I

haven't slept for two nights. Your mother is frantic to talk to you, through me."

"If we can prove it to you, Harry," Conan Doyle said, "will you stop your testimony before Congress tomorrow?"

Harry shrugged. "I'll vote the straight Spiritualist ticket."

"Then come to our hotel room. Now. I swear to you," he said softly, "there *is* another world. I've seen it."

For a moment, no one spoke. Inside all of us somewhere is the unspoken belief that there must be more to life than the little we know of it. The deeper we pry into science, the more we understand that such tremendous order in the physical world must come from somewhere; it is impossible that Creation, the Big Bang, was pure chance, a roll of the dice.

Bess had moved to her husband's side.

"You have to go, Harry."

He still hesitated.

"Well?" Sir Arthur prodded.

Harry turned to Lady Conan Doyle.

"If you promise you won't do it naked," he said, and smiled.

In the darkened hotel room, lit only by two lonely candles, her hand moved and picked up a pencil. Then, with spasmodic jerks, as if controlled from beyond her being, the hand struck the table three times.

"Who are you?" Lady Conan Doyle inquired, not in fear, not in doubt, but simply. "Who are you? Do you believe in God?"

Again, her hand struck the table. Then it moved slowly to the tablet lying open in front of her, and drew a vertical line. It moved again, and drew a horizontal line through it. The sign of the cross.

A candle snuffed out, suddenly. There was a slight breeze from the open window—perhaps that was it.

"I feel her presence," Sir Arthur said quietly. He was seated next to his wife at the round table, Harry completing the trinity.

Suddenly, Lady Conan Doyle's hand began to move over the notepad, writing, writing in beautifully spaced words, evenly spaced lines, although her eyes were closed.

"Oh, my darling boy," her hand was writing; the pages exist to this day, it is all there, visible to be read by anyone. "Thank God, thank God, at last I am through."

Lady Conan Doyle's lips were moving, reading the words as they were written, reading although her eyes were shut in self-induced sleep.

"I want to talk to my own beloved boy—Harry— Harry—there is a terrible danger, you have angered many on this side—you must stop, you don't realize—there is horror here, there are evil forces here, who want to drag you over the divide—stop, Harry, stop. Goodbye. God's blessing on you all . . ." The pencil fell from her fingers. She leaned back in her chair, exhausted. Her husband took her hand and massaged it as, slowly, slowly, her eyes opened and she came out of her sleep.

Harry had risen quietly and turned his back to them. They waited then, in the plush hotel room in the capital city of the United States, for his re-action to the words that might have come from an even greater Nation.

"My mother would have cut off her right arm before she'd make the sign of the cross." He was trying to control his hurt. He crossed to the table and indicated the writing. "Another little thing. Mama couldn't write English. Yiddish, Hungarian, German, sure. English, no."

He turned away.

"Perhaps she learned in Heaven," Sir Arthur said.

"What have they got up there? City College?"

"Harry—!"

"That's another thing. Who got my mother to call me Harry?" He smiled to himself at the thought. "I tried for thirty years. Ehrich, she called me. 'Ehrincha' "—unconsciously his voice took on Cecilia Weiss's Yiddish rhythm—" 'you shouldn't be ashamed, it's a nice name.' In Budapest, I said, it's a nice name, on Delancey Street call me Harry.

'All right, Ehrich,' she said, 'I'll try I should remember, Ehrincha.' "

Jean Conan Doyle had turned white. She had tried to help; she had not expected mockery.

"Then I am just another crook?" she asked.

Harry put a hand on her shoulder. She pulled away.

"Of course you're not," he said, as kindly as he could say it at this moment. "You and Arthur want so much to think you're talking to your son who was killed in the war . . ." How could he say it without hurting them? "You know what the subconscious can do to the mind. You want it so much, it seems possible."

"Don't you?"

"Goddammit, I want it so much I tried to die! I want it so much I'm still waiting to hear one word from my mother, one word I'll know is from her. I'll believe, I'll believe, if I hear it, but I won't. Tonight was the finish. It convinced me that even honest people can't get through, nobody can. We're stuck here on this side and *there is no other side*."

Conan Doyle had risen to his feet. "All right," he said, "don't believe. But for God's sake, listen to her warning. I've been through this. Three of my friends have died, and the warnings were not this clear. Call me a fake, but call me your friend. Don't take the risk, Harry. Stop your atheistic crusade." He was shaking now, the intensity of his feelings almost too much. Couldn't this fool understand?

Harry reached into his pocket and pulled out the page he had torn out of the book, on his way over that evening.

" 'Rubbish, Watson, rubbish!' " he read. " 'What have we to do with stalking corpses who can only be held in their graves with stakes driven through their hearts? It's pure lunacy. This agency stands flatfooted on the ground, and there it must remain. No ghosts need apply.' " He looked up from the page. "That's from *The Adventure of the Sussex Vampire*. What happened to the fellow who wrote that? His brain turned to mush?"

"Get out," said Conan Doyle angrily.

"Come on, Arthur, have a little common sense, have a—"

"You have insulted me, you have insulted my wife, but more than that, you have insulted the Almighty Himself!"

"Horse shit!" Harry looked heavenward. "Am I getting through?" he inquired.

And he turned and left the room and his friendship.

# ACT TEN

~~~~~~~~~~

BESS had his clothes spread out on the bed. She was folding them mechanically now, the hurt within her too great to allow for concentration. Or perhaps she didn't want to look at his suits, fearing some further discovery.

Harry entered angrily from the hall, his resentment having grown on the four-block walk from the Carlton Hotel. He yanked off his tie.

"Idiots," he said. He flung off his jacket.

"Did you and Mama have a nice talk?" Bess knew she didn't really care any more.

"What turns intelligent people into fools?" Harry was too involved in his own feelings to notice her attitude. "Nobody's ever going to communicate from the Beyond!"

"Not like they do from New York, anyway."

He turned. Bess was holding out two letters to him.

"I was going through your suits to send them to be pressed," she said, trying not to show the hurt but hoping he saw it anyway. "I could have saved myself the trouble. These seem to be from Daisy White, they steamed your pants already."

Who told her to go through my pockets, Harry asked himself unreasonably. How could he have left them there? Schmuck!

"Excuse me, may I turn down the bed?"

The night maid had entered, unnoticed.

"Sure," Harry said. "We may not use it, but go ahead."

He crossed toward Bess, lowering his voice so the maid wouldn't hear.

"I can't make her stop writing, can I?"

Bess was holding up the letters again.

"Do you have to keep everything she writes? Who is she, Shakespeare?"

She ripped the letters in half and tossed them in the wastebasket, then walked out on the terrace. The maid seemed to be listening; why give her an earful?

Harry followed. It was bad, he knew, how bad he wasn't sure. He had been a fool. But wild horses wouldn't make him admit it.

"You knew you weren't marrying Little Lord Fauntleroy!" he shouted. That was the best thing to do, shout.

"Shhh," said Bess. "Sure, I knew, but I didn't figure on the Jewish Don Juan."

She leaned against the railing, looking off at the lighted dome of the Capitol in the distance. This time, she told herself, she wasn't going to cry. This time. This last time.

"What are you gonna do, leave me again?" Harry wanted to know, searching for a way. "When I have to testify before Congress?" What wife could leave a husband who had to testify before Congress?

"I don't know, Harry. I honest to God don't know." But she knew. If she had any pride at all, this had to be the end. "But I'm not going with you to hold your hand." And still, she didn't cry. *Mazeltov*, she told herself.

Inside, in the bedroom, the night maid crossed silently, unnoticed, to the wastebasket.

She bent down and picked up the torn letters and stuffed them into the pocket of her apron.

And left.

"FORTUNE Telling. Hearings before the Subcommittee on Judiciary of the Committee on the District of Columbia. House of Representatives. Sixty-Ninth Congress. First Session. On H.R. 8989." The transcript is still available from the Government Printing Office, but the cold print gives little hint of the passions involved, the shouting, the turmoil. The hearing room was packed with advocates of both sides, and neither was noted for restraint. It took on all the aspects of a show, a performance. A vaudeville. A Congress.

"Walter . . . Walter . . . are you there?" The falsetto voice was Harry's, as he imitated Margery. Three members of the Congressional committee had been persuaded—nay, had volunteered—to be blindfolded and seated at a table with Houdini, so he could demonstrate what actually went on in the dark at one of Margery's seances. Everything short of stripping naked, of course, which at that time was deemed impossible in the sacred halls of Congress.

"Dammit, Margery, I was busy, what the hell do you want?" Harry had modified Walter's vocabulary in deference to his surroundings.

"We have unbelievers today . . . give us a sign that you are here."

Underneath the table, in full view of the spectators but unseen by his blindfolded subjects, Harry slipped his foot out of his shoe. His sock had been cut half away, leaving his educated toes free. With them, he picked up a dinner bell from under the table and rang it loudly. Then he picked up a tambourine and sent it rolling out into the hearing room as the spectators burst into laughter.

"Goddammit, Houdini," he said in Walter's gruff voice, "hold the table down or I'll make it fly away!"

Harry's hands were held firmly by two of the seated Congressmen. He quickly lowered his head beneath the table without their perceiving it, and then upended the table on his unsuspecting guests, who leaped to their feet, startled, and then pulled off their blindfolds and joined in the general hilarity. The spectators were applauding now, but the applause was mixed with jeering and hissing from the Spiritualists in the audience. The Congressmen returned to their places on the dais and the chairman gaveled for order. The booing continued.

"Houdini, you are the Anti-Christ!"

It was a sharp, piercing voice lifted above the din. Harry whirled. A woman was standing up among the spectators, pointing at him accusingly, a tall woman dressed severely, a woman with commanding presence.

There was a hush.

"Jesus was persecuted, and now we of the Spiritualist religion are being persecuted!" The words rang through the hearing room with biblical intensity. "I am a minister of the Lord, God has given me the gift, I am the Reverend Le Veyne—"

She was interrupted by a wave of applause from among her followers; the Reverend Le Veyne was from Massachusetts, but her reputation was nationwide. This was an age when religion received almost as much attention in the press as baseball. She barely acknowledged the applause with a nod, and swept on with her rhetoric: "—and I say again, you are the Devil's messenger!"

The shouts broke out again, the applause, the jeers. The chairman had a difficult time making the gavel heard. Harry waited patiently until the room was quiet.

"Everyone knows the famous Reverend Le Veyne," he said. "I would like you to meet the Reverend Frances Raud." And, dramatically, the Great Houdini pointed to a figure in widow's black seated among the spectators, a veil covering her face. The chair next to hers was empty, the chair he had hoped Bess would occupy.

"Reverend Raud," he asked theatrically, "are you an ordained minister of the Spiritualist Church?"

"If I ain't I'm out eleven bucks," said Minnie, throwing back her veil and tossing her certificate of ordination on the committee's table. "I also juggle and whistle Dixie," she said. It was her biggest audience in years, how could she resist milking another laugh?

Again the chairman had to gavel for order.

"Mr. Houdini," he said impatiently, "what relevance does this have to the—"

"Congressman, I think you'll find this very relevant evidence. Reverend Raud is in my employ." He turned back to Minnie. "Have you visited the Reverend Le Veyne on my instructions?"

"I had the ten-dollar seance," Minnie said. "Spoke to both my dead children. Since I never been married and never had the pleasure of getting pregnant, it was a nice surprise for all of us."

"I never saw that woman before in my life!" It was a screech now; the Reverend Le Veyne had lost her temper completely.

"I got your signature on my receipt for my ten bucks," Minnie shouted back; not one to be intimidated by some second banana in the audience. "Had you make it out to 'F. Raud'—Fraud! Strange you didn't recognize your own name."

A shout of laughter from some of the spectators. Harry seized the occasion to reach inside his jacket and pull out the package of bills he had brought with him. He tossed it on the committee table, greenbacks spilling out in front of the startled Congressmen.

"There's ten thousand dollars in cash," he called above the din. "Any medium in this room who can produce a manifestation I can't prove is a phony gets to take it home!"

Pandemonium. The shouting, the jeering, the gavel, rose to a crescendo. In the rear of the hearing room, a door opened. It was Bess. She had fought a struggle with herself, and lost. She saw Harry in the middle of the hearing room, embattled, fighting to be heard above the din, and she knew she had to be here. Being Harry, he might try to bring down the government if she didn't stop him. She would leave right after the hearing, she told herself, but, for the moment, she allowed the sergeant-at-arms to lead her to the seat beside Minnie.

"Mr. Houdini, you have already attacked the Presidency." The chairman, a hard-bitten politician, was afraid the proceedings were getting away from him. "You have charged that President Coolidge has conducted Spiritualist seances in the White House, and that the widow of Warren G. Harding has attempted to communicate with her dead husband through Spiritualist mediums. Do you realize that Spiritualism is a religion protected by the Constitution? Are you attacking the Constitution?"

The chairman hadn't been taken in by the vaudeville performance. Let's get this bastard on the record, he thought; there ought to be some votes in that.

"No, sir."

"Then, sir, are you attacking religion itself?"

"No, sir. My father was a rabbi. For hundreds of years my forebears were rabbis. I believe in Almighty God." He was subdued now. Ehrich was speaking. "But I do not believe the disembodied spirit can come back, even for a Republican President. There are only two kinds of mediums: those who are mental degenerates and ought to be under observation, and those who are moral degenerates and deliberate cheats and frauds."

Now it was all about him, the hissing, the jeering, the shouts, but he saw Bess, and he felt relieved. Maybe it was going to be all right between them. She was here, wasn't she?

"Atheist!" they were shouting. "Liar!"

"You have been sent by the devil to destroy our church!" The Reverend Le Veyne was on her feet again, dominating the entire room with her presence, her carefully cultivated voice of Doom. It was her living. "Yes, to destroy our church, just as Judas destroyed Christ—and Judas was a Jew, too!"

A gasp from her audience. After all, Representa-

tive Sol Bloom, who had introduced the bill, was
Jewish. This hit a little too close to the kind of
truth seldom heard on Capitol Hill.

"There, it's out in the open," cried the Reverend
defiantly, the mask dropped at last. "This is a
Jewish plot against Jesus Christ, and it's not the
first one!"

Harry had started toward her. Bess was half
out of her chair, but Minnie pulled her down.

"Houdini," shouted the Reverend Le Veyne, in
righteous wrath, "how dare you call our ministers
degenerates? Your testimony is worthless because
your character is worthless. *You* are the de-
generate." And she opened her purse and took out
the torn letters, the letters she had been given only
that morning, and waved them above her head for
all to see. She knew it was melodrama. That's what
she was famous for, that's why they came to hear
her sermons. Otherwise, they would go to the
movies and watch Rin Tin Tin. "A good Christian
woman gave me these letters, proof that you are a
shameless adulterer who has had sexual relations
with a woman not your wife!" She paused, knowing
her audience would want to savor that. "How can
you stand in judgment on a Christian church?
You're a vile beast, it's all here in black and white,
I place these letters in evidence!" And with a
dramatic gesture, she threw them on the committee table as the spectators erupted in shouts
and applause, the tide having swung toward Jesus.

The chairman angrily gaveled them into silence again. The Jewish vote was important, too. How did he get into these things?

"Do you wish to reply?" he asked Harry.

"Yes, sir. It's true."

A startled murmur. Bess, who had been watching him, looked away. There was no room for pretending after that.

"I would like to present a witness in my own defense," Harry said.

"That's your privilege."

"May I have my wife placed under oath?"

She looked up then, surprised.

"Will Mrs. Houdini rise and come forward to be sworn in?" the chairman asked. Bess hesitated. The Jewish Don Juan, what did he want?

"Mrs. Houdini?"

Finally, she got to her feet and crossed slowly to face the Congressman.

"Raise your right hand and place your left hand on the Bible." I hope the Old Testament is in that book, too, Harry thought. "Do you swear to tell the truth, the whole truth, and nothing but the truth, so help you God?"

"I do." Bess's voice was barely audible. She let Harry lead her by the arm and seat her in the chair. He stood for a moment, watching her.

Then, very quietly, he asked, "Are you a Christian?"

"Yes."

"Am I a Jew?"

"Yes."

"How long have we lived together, sharing the good, sharing the bad, Jew and Gentile, side by side?"

She closed her eyes, thinking how long it had been, how very long, since the roller coaster at Coney Island.

"Years," she said. "Years and years and years."

"Do you still love me?"

She couldn't look up at him. She couldn't answer.

"Bess, you're under oath. Do you still love me?"

He waited silently. It was difficult for her to speak, but she managed it finally.

"Yes."

"My God," said Harry, "she's crying again."

And he put his arms about her as she rose from the chair, and started to lead her back to her seat.

"That doesn't mean anything, she's his wife!" They were shouting again, jeering. Bess didn't hear, didn't care. "He's still an atheist! Anti-Christ!"

A hand stopped her, a hand clutching at her coat. She looked up and saw the face of the Reverend Le Veyne, twisted with anger.

"Mrs. Houdini!" The shout rose above the din. "Your husband is a Jew and a fornicator!"

Bess turned and looked her squarely in the eye.

"I know," she said. "You should be so lucky."


Rain pelted the streets of Detroit, that Halloween

week in 1926. The Great Houdini opened his Spirit Exposé in the city of the automobile, and the crowds came, drawn not only by his performance but by the notoriety of his appearance before Congress. The atmosphere was ominous, the crowds not always friendly, and in Washington the bill Harry had fought so hard for was defeated. Fortunetellers and mediums would be allowed to continue to operate in the nation's capital, with the same chance of reaching the Beyond as a bill to cut Congressional salaries had of passing the House of Representatives.

Harry did not let up. He intensified his attacks onstage and continued to lecture at universities.

Two prominent mediums announced they had received messages from the Beyond predicting Houdini's imminent demise. Harry said he would have been surprised if they hadn't. They must have a Western Union form Up There by now.

Only to Bess, they weren't amusing. She was late for the theater this night, having paused to do some belated shopping, and for the first time she realized how much Halloween celebrated Death: the skeletons, the ghosts, the grinning faces. They could be amusing only to children; no young man believes he will ever die, she remembered that from somewhere, and huddled her coat about her.

Coming down the alley to the stage door, a black cat crossed her path. Harry would walk around the block and go in the front entrance, she thought to herself. And then deny it, she thought again, and smiled. The doorman waved her inside and she started to cross the stage, still deserted at that hour except for the hanging cutouts that were part of the Halloween stage setting. Accidentally, she brushed a cardboard cutout of a witch on a broomstick and set it swinging.

"Sorry, Mama," she said aloud, and smiled again.

As she approached the star dressing room, she stopped short, A girl was coming out, a girl in a revealing dress and a fur choker.

"Happy Halloween," Bess said quietly.

Daisy turned.

"Oh, hi, Bess. Just dropped by to say hello."

"From New York? You could have written."

"I'm opening across the street."

"Really? You'll have to get a bicycle." Bess brushed by her, hoping she hadn't revealed how badly she was hurt. It was done, she had thought, dead and buried, it was a part of her life with Harry she would never have to face again. But it wasn't. Obviously.

"Bess?" Daisy hadn't moved. It was something that had to be said. "Believe me, nothing. I tried. Not a goddam thing."

"You forget," Bess told her, "I'm a mind reader." And she entered the dressing room.

Harry was dressing for the act. He looked up, surprised.

"Bess! Didn't expect you so soon."

"I'll bet." She tried to control the panic she felt. Things were happening before she could anticipate them. Everything seemed planned, organized from somewhere; the vaudeville was building to the big moment. Next to shut, they called it. The headline act always went on next to last, so that if the audience called it back for encores, the final act could be trimmed, and the show would finish on time.

Next to shut, she felt, unreasonably, the show was finishing.

"My God, Harry, don't you have better taste?" Bess set down the packages and removed her hat. Her hands were trembling; she hoped he wouldn't notice. "After the hearing, you promised me it was all over."

Harry looked up innocently.

"Daisy?" He laughed. "Bess, I swear—"

"On your mother's grave? I met *her*, too." She knew she wasn't making sense, but she didn't care. "Are there any more?"

"Now you're getting hysterical." Harry turned to the mirror to fasten his bow tie.

"Wouldn't you? In front of Congress, I stripped myself naked, I have no more pride, no more secrets. You know exactly how I feel, and yet you let her come here and—"

"I didn't *let* her!"

"She walked through the wall?"

Harry grabbed her by the shoulders.

"For God's sake, Bess, this isn't like you! What's happened?"

She had to tell him, even though she knew he'd laugh at her.

"I've been having nightmares, Harry." He laughed. "Nightmares . . . that hearing . . . those faces . . . that woman. And they won. Congress didn't pass the law against them, they won. They have some kind of power, I don't know what. Suppose they really can see something we can't see? Harry, don't do the Water Torture tonight. I'm not sure I want to see you again, and I'm frightened to death I'll never see you again."

There was a knock at the door. Harry turned, annoyed.

"Who is it?"

"Jack Price," came the young voice. "We're here for the interview, Mr. Houdini."

Harry groaned helplessly.

"Kids from the university," he explained to Bess. "I invited them after the lecture. I'll get rid of them fast."

She didn't seem to hear. She sat down in front of the makeup table and started to remove her jewelry. It was time to be a performer again.

Harry opened the door and admitted two young men, a little ill at ease at being backstage in the presence of a headliner, but eager and excited.

"Come in, come in," Harry told them. "Sorry I've only got a few minutes for the interview. "Oh,

Bess." She turned. "This is Jack Price, of the school paper." He indicated the shorter one, eyeglasses, obviously the student. "And this is Harold—who?"

"Harold Graham, sir, of the boxing team." Six foot. Varsity letter proudly on his sweater.

"Oh yes, Slugger Graham. And this is my wife." He turned to Bess. "You're still my wife?"

She pretended to busy herself at the makeup table.

"I'm not sure. After everything that's happened, I'm still not sure I really know you." She didn't want the students to hear; no young man believes he will ever die, how could they understand? What she felt had little to do with what she was saying. Would they understand that, the young people who were taking over the world? She was frightened by the Unknown, and one of them was her husband.

"Harold heard your standing offer." The student had been speaking; neither Bess nor Harry was paying much attention. Harry had returned to putting on his jacket. "Is it true anybody can slug you in the stomach twice without hurting you?"

"Bess," Harry said to her, "will you listen? Nothing's going to happen tonight."

"We thought it could lead off the story," the student continued.

"Does the offer still stand, Mr. Houdini?" The big kid in the varsity sweater was rubbing his knuckles.

"Sure, sure." He turned back to his wife. "I'm not going to beg you!"

"Okay, so don't beg!"

"Okay, I won't!" He turned away and simultaneously Slugger Graham belted him in the pit of the stomach with all of his well-conditioned strength. It felt like a fireball exploding inside. Harry gasped, choked, gagged; the pain was incredible as he doubled up and fell to the floor. There hadn't been that split second to tense the abdominal muscles Harry had trained to absorb such blows.

"My God!" Bess rushed to him, kneeling beside his pained body, some bell in the back of her mind tolling. Not like this, not like this, she thought, as she unfastened his tie, his collar.

Harry Houdini forced himself to his feet, clutching at a table momentarily for support.

"It's all right, Bess, it's all right," he said, as he managed a smile for the two foolish young men who had probably planned it just this way—show up the big-shot old-timer for what he was, maybe make the wire services. He straightened himself and stood erect. No one would ever know the effort it took.

"You got another one coming, Slugger," he said.

"Harry!" Even as she said it, Bess knew it was hopeless. Maier Samuel Weiss's son. Too proud to live.

Slugger stared at his companion, startled. The

old guy should have been flat on his ass, the look said, should I give him another shot?

"Come on, college boy," Harry taunted. "I can take a dozen punks like you."

Twenty-three fights, fourteen knockouts. Slugger had his pride, too. He swung another tremendous right to the pit of the old boy's stomach—he asked for it, didn't he? But this time Harry was ready. The blow hit tensed, solid muscle. Harry staggered a bit, but remained upright.

"Nothing," he said. He had to get them out of there right away. He held out his hand. "See you after the show, I gotta dress."

"You got rocks in your stomach," Slugger said admiringly, as he shook Harry's hand.

"Thanks. Yours are a little higher up."

The two young men laughed. It would make a good story anyway, Boxing Team Loses Another; maybe he wore a board under his belt; Houdini was an old fox, he had all kinds of tricks; they'd have a lot of good lies to tell when they got back on campus.

The moment the door closed, Harry clutched at the chair behind him and sank to his knees, coughing. He put his handkerchief to his mouth as he doubled up on the floor again. Bess knelt to him, trying not to panic. How had she known in advance it was going to happen? So it couldn't happen, she was being foolish, he was hurt, that's all,

she'd get him to lie down, he'd be all right, he had
to be all right.

"Harry, you're coughing blood!" She had seen
it on his handkerchief, the vital red stain, and the
panic began now, as she struggled to get him to his
feet, to get him to the couch.

"I'm all right, it's nothing, it's nothing," he
mumbled.

She put him down on the couch and ran to wet
a towel at the sink.

"You're not going on tonight. I'm going to get
a doctor!"

He was coughing again.

"And have it all over town? I'll be finished. The
Great Houdini! A college boy! Who'll walk through
my dressing-room wall?"

She was back, wiping his face with the damp
towel, trying to think quickly. How could she get
him to cancel the foolish performance without
arousing that unreasoning pride again? What's so
important about being a magician?

"I really wasn't going to walk out again," she
said, "no matter what. I have to love you. I said
it in front of Congress."

"Who do I have to say it in front of so you'll
believe me?"

"You? You're you. You don't have to say it. I'm
supposed to know."

He reached up and grasped her hand.

"Believe, Bess, believe. Until the day I die. No, even after I die. Believe."

She held him to her. Why don't we go away, she thought, anyplace we don't find ourselves always talking about death?

"Don't go out on the stage. Please, Harry, let me call a doctor."

"My God, she's crying again," Harry said.

The stage manager was knocking at the door. "Ten minutes!" he shouted.

"I'll be there," Harry called. He looked at Bess. "We'll be there!" he said.


"Pomp and Circumstance," the orchestra was playing, his theme. How appropriate, Bess thought, as she stood there onstage, helpless, helpless in the tights and blouse of a magician's assistant. Even at her age they were expected of her. Her figure was still good, she told herself; from the audience they could still tell she was a female. The red-coated attendants had fastened Harry's bare ankles into the stocks, the stocks that were gimmicked so that, despite a thorough check by the committee, Harry could free his feet while he was locked under five feet of water. Now he was hoisted in midair. She knew the effort of will it must have cost him to wave at the audience as he was suspended upside down, fifteen feet above the stage, and then lowered to the top of the Water Torture. He grasped the edge of the tank tightly, and then the pain became too much. He felt faint; Harry Houdini only performed sure things, and the water below waited too quietly for him within the cabinet that looked like a coffin, a coffin with one glass wall.

A roll of the drums. A cymbal crashed. For one hesitant moment he thought of surrender. Call it off, miss one performance. And then the audience was clapping, rhythmically, impatiently, what was he waiting for, on with the show!

He signaled the attendants, one of them good old Jim Collins, who had taken Franz Kukol's place a dozen years ago, and they dropped him into the tank, water cascading over its sides. He went down, down, all the way under, the pressure pounding at his eardrums, water forcing itself into his nostrils as he dropped lower and lower until his fingers touched the bottom. Through the glass he could see the footlights, upside down, the audience a dark mass of eyes staring at him. He was completely submerged under five and a half feet of water, bound and fettered at the ankles, they could all see him. The pressure on his lungs was almost more than he could bear this time, the pain in his gut numbing his brain, bubbles rising from his mouth. It was certainly worth the price of admission tonight, even if he got out alive.

Bess signaled for the drape to be pulled up about the dripping tank. Another roll of the drums, and she turned and smiled at the audience.

Then it happened. She had felt it would, so it

couldn't be happening. But the little boy had broken his arm falling from that bicycle, hadn't he? This was all too neat, all the predictions had said it would happen. But why here, who or what had planned it so theatrically? Was God in Show Business?

"He can't get out!" A stagehand, high in the flies. He knew that by now Harry should have sprung the gimmick with his feet, he should be turning around underwater with his contortionist's skill, ready to climb out of the tank, that's what they paid him for, to escape, he should be escaping.

"He's not coming up!"

They had faked panic so many times to arouse the audience and give the Milk Can escape a sock finish that Bess felt she had lived through it all before. But this time the panic was real, she was screaming for the drape around the tank to be dropped, the main curtain was being pulled to deny the audience a final thrill, the house lights came up, someone was running out with a fire axe, and there was Harry, in the tank, moving, still moving feebly, trying to give the signal to be hauled out, thumbs up, that was the distress signal, thumbs up, ironically. They started to pull him up, his body swaying from side to side against the walls of the tank, and Bess never forgot that she could see the cutout of the witch on the broomstick, behind the tank, swinging slowly to and fro, to and fro.

Harry Houdini died in Grace Hospital, Detroit, of a ruptured appendix, October 31, 1926. Bess was at his side. He had lingered for several days, slipping in and out of consciousness. Everyone knew he was waiting for Halloween to make his final exit.

It made such a good headline.

# NEXT TO SHUT

SHE remembered tumbling down the stairs, when Mama's picture fell; her ankle must have twisted under her, she hit her head, and it had taken all of Minnie's strength to get her onto the couch, and call the doctor. The last thing Bess could remember seeing was the Halloween jack o'lantern outside the window, grinning, as she rolled headlong down the steps.

She was better now. Her ankle had been taped, after a few days she had been able to walk with a cane, the lump on her forehead had subsided. But she couldn't shake from her mind the memory of having been pushed down the stairs. Harry had been dead two years; Mama over a decade. But Bess couldn't avoid the feeling, whenever she looked at the mantel, that Mama's picture was going to

tilt at an angle again, the clock was going to stop,
the music box was going to fly open and play.
Had it all been in her mind? Or not?

Good Lord, she thought, I'm beginning to think
like the Reverend Le Veyne. Maybe I should go
and have my palm read. Harry must be laughing
at me. Then she realized she had given herself
away by thinking that; she must stop it. For two
years she had been pestered by fakes and phonies
who had messages from him in the Great Beyond.
She must stop thinking of Harry as being around
somewhere, smiling at her foolishness; that made
it even more foolish, made her no better than the
spiritualists.

Then the nightmares started. The same nightmares she had had before Detroit. The only way
to avoid them was not to sleep. Minnie found her
at three o'clock one morning, in her nightgown,
holding the music box in her lap in the living room
and listening as it played the melody of "Rosabelle,"
exactly as it had the night Harry had given it to
her, the night of Nathan's wedding.

She had let Minnie guide her upstairs to bed,
but she knew what she had to do.

"Minnie—"

"Go to sleep, I'll be in the next room."

"I can't sleep. Look in the phone book, see if
the First Spiritualist Church has a number."

"Why would they need a phone? They got two
operators on a Ouija board."

"Look anyway. I want to reach Reverend Ford."

"It's three o'clock in the morning. I don't think he makes house calls."

"I bet he'll make this one. Call him as soon as they open."

He came that afternoon, in the rain—it was raining again in New York. Bess had waited impatiently all day. She was so nervous that Minnie had insisted on mixing her a martini, forcing it on her like medicine, which in those Prohibition days was the way martinis tasted.

The second martini was Bess's idea.

Minnie admitted the young minister at the front door, taking his umbrella and his cane—he was a punctilious dresser.

"Come in, come in, don't catch cold," she said.

"It's miserable out." He shook the rain from his overcoat.

"It's miserable in, too; we're outta gin. Can I take your coat?"

He handed it to her as he looked around. The living room was filled with Harry's presence, his mementoes, his photographs.

"Thank you for calling me," he said politely.

"Don't thank me, I just work here." Minnie still thought it was a bad idea. "I'm a disappointed atheist. I don't believe in sin and I'm not gettin' any."

The line went over pretty well in vaudeville, but it didn't seem to get much from ministers, she noted.

She ushered him into the living room and called, "Bess, it's the fella from the graveyard."

Bess was already coming down the stairs, having heard the bell. She was leaning on her cane, her face flushed. Now that he was here, she wasn't too certain she wanted to see him.

"Hello, Reverend." At least be polite.

"Mrs. Houdini." He noted the cane. "Did you have an accident?"

"Somebody pushed her down the stairs," Minnie said, "but there wasn't anybody there. Happens all the time at your church, I'm sure."

Bess reached the bottom of the steps and crossed directly to Ford.

"Are you a phony?" she asked. What the hell. Why beat around the bush? "You can tell me. I used to be in the business."

He seemed to be expecting her question.

"I don't know," he said quietly.

"That's a hell of an answer."

"She doesn't really drink," Minnie apologized quickly, "just two little martinis and a shot of cough medicine, she's not responsible."

She tried to get Bess to sit down—you didn't let a minister see you were unsteady on your feet— but Bess motioned her away.

"Yes, I am," she said. "I'm a little drunk, *and* responsible. So I can say what I feel." She took a deep breath, and the room seemed to swim a little. "You'll excuse me, Reverend, I still ache for him at night, and if you're another fourflusher, I'm gonna expose you like we did all the others, I'm gonna drive you and your phony church right into the East River."

"Perhaps I had better leave." He was turning away when her voice stopped him.

"Don't leave! You think I'd let one chance in a million pass?" She was crossing to the mantel now, crossing to his photograph, crossing to his music box. "He got out of straitjackets, didn't he? You know how? He could dislocate both his shoulders, that's how you get out of a straitjacket. Would you do it even if you could? But *he did it*. They sealed him in a coffin and held him under water for an hour and a half, the doctors said there wasn't enough oxygen for five minutes, but *he did it*. All his life, all he wanted to do was escape. How can I be sure he's finally stopped trying?" She paused, swaying again, and her hand went to her forehead, and she realized it was damp with perspiration. "Minnie, isn't there any more gin?"

"If there was, I'd drink it myself. I've never seen you like this."

"I've never been like this."

Ford had waited, silently, for her to finish. But she wasn't done. She turned to him.

"Go on, Reverend. What's the message for me from the Great Beyond? But remember—*I know what it is*. Harry and I agreed, when I held him in my arms at the hospital in Detroit, Harry and I agreed on a message no lying seance fakers could possibly figure out, because the only place they could find it was in our hearts. Only if I hear it word for word will I believe." She was swaying again. "Oh, boy, I'm a little dizzy."

Minnie helped her into a chair.

"That cough medicine'll do it everytime," Minnie said diplomatically. Reverend Ford was crossing to retrieve his hat and coat.

"I told you, I have no message from your husband," he said.

Bess was eyeing him watchfully. The way she thought Harry might have.

"Clever," she said. "What's the next move?"

"To leave. You're in no condition to listen to reason."

"What the hell does reason have to do with it? If you talked to Mama, *prove it*." That's what he had told her at the cemetery, wasn't it? "Does the name Cecilia mean anything to you?" Reverend, would you really like to know what it means to me?

"I can't prove it," he said. "I can believe it; only you can prove it. I have no idea what her message means."

"I'll know. Try me."

"It was just one word. Well, two."

"What words?" She was smiling. She had him. He had to make a stab at it now, and fail, like all the others.

" 'I forgive,' " he said.

Something was pushing her down the stairs again, screaming in her ear, trying to get her attention. She was falling, falling, she had to stop! She was on her feet, shouting to Minnie: "Get him out of here! Right away!"

She turned and started to limp toward the stairway; she'd forgotten her cane, forgotten everything. How could he have known? Was it a wild guess?

"Mrs. Houdini—"

"Out, goddammit!"

"You heard the lady, Reverend," Minnie told him, glad it was over now. She had died a thousands deaths for Bess in the last ten minutes.

"Wait!" Bess had turned, halfway up the steps. She pointed directly at Reverend Ford.

"Tomorrow," she said. "Tomorrow morning. In broad daylight. And I want a committee. I want the toughest damn committee you ever heard of!"

The committee consisted of John W. Stafford, Associate Editor of *Scientific American*; Rea Jaure, a hard-bitten, cynical sob sister from the sensational New York tabloid of the twenties, the *Daily Graphic*; Harry W. Zander, a reputable correspondent for the United Press; Francis R. Post, a Wall Street broker who took down the entire seance in shorthand; and the two toughest skeptics of all, Minnie Chester and Bess Houdini.

It was broad daylight outside, but the curtains were drawn in Bess's living room, two candles

supplying the only illumination. The group was
seated in chairs in a circle in the center of the room,
Bess lying on the couch with her ankle propped up,
Minnie at her side.

Arthur Ford was understandably nervous. Sometimes, he said, it was impossible to make contact;
there was no way to know in advance, and this
assemblage might be too forbidding. Bess smiled.
Excuses, excuses. She had heard them all.

The Reverend Ford was to go on to make an
international reputation in his field; he would later
allow Bishop Pike to speak to his dead son, a conversation the Bishop attested to on national tele-
vision before he died mysteriously, on a journey
to the Holy Land. Ford was to write several books
on his experiences, and several more would be
written about Arthur Ford. But on this day, he was
relatively unknown, and confronting the reputation
of Harry Houdini, who had called all spiritualists
either mental or moral degenerates. It was the kind
of a spot, as they used to say in vaudeville, you
wouldn't give to a leopard.

Bess was watching him closely. Ford had never
given any intimation of anything but sincerity; he
was not interested in the money, including Harry's
own, that was then on deposit for anyone pro-
ducing authentic psychic phenomena. His behavior
was that of a religious man who believed in his
religion. Bess had not been able to figure out his
angle, until she decided that was it: his angle was

that he didn't have an angle, which made him unique in his profession. She sipped at the glass of ginger ale Minnie had given her—no more martinis, thank you—and watched, in some amusement, as the Reverend Arthur Ford tried to persuade his tough-minded audience to give him the benefit of the doubt that exists, somewhere, in all of us.

"I will try to reach my contact in the Other World, an old college friend named Fletcher who died a long time ago." They tried to suppress their smiles, the newspapermen who had seen everything, who were already formulating their mocking stories for the late editions.

"He is my guide into Eternity," Reverend Ford said, loosening his collar and leaning back, trying to relax, in his chair. "I know most of you are doubters, but please try to keep an open mind. As Shakespeare said, 'There are more things in Heaven and Earth, Horatio, than are dreamt of in your Philosophy.' "

Bess smiled. Shakespeare, yet.

The Reverend Ford's eyes were closing. His voice trailed off. His breathing became deeper, more regular, slower. His body twitched, convulsively, once, twice. His face was deep in shadow. Then, a voice issued from his lips, a voice far different from his own. There was no trace of the Southern accent, and it seemed somehow disembodied, far away, yet here.

"Hello." The voice was strained, as if it some-

how felt the doubt in that room. "Hello, this is
Fletcher."

Rea Jaure snickered. Her specialty was rape,
adultery, and divorce, usually illustrated with
composographs, the *Graphic*'s specialty, a photograph doctored to depict whoever doing whatever
made a good story. This morning was a waste of
time.

"A man who says he is Ehrich Weiss is here,"
said the voice. "He tells me to say, 'Hello, Bess,
sweetheart. I want you to remember exactly what
we said in the hospital, in Detroit.'"

Of course, Reverend Ford knew a message had
been arranged in the hospital, Bess thought wearily.
Everyone knew. Just as they knew Harry's name
was Ehrich Weiss.

The voice was continuing.

"Now he says, 'Have you any message for me?'"

"How about 'Horse manure,'" Minnie murmured, reaching to pour some ginger ale for herself for want of something stronger.

"Shhh," Bess tried to quiet her.

"I can talk," Minnie insisted. "I'm an ordained
minister."

The voice spoke again.

"He says, 'No, Minnie, you were a bouncer in a
house of ill repute.'"

"Jesus Christ!"

The glass of ginger ale fell from Minnie's nerve-
less fingers, smashing on the floor. How the hell

could anyone have known *that* line?

She started to mop up the mess with a napkin. Her hands were shaking.

"What is the message he has for *me*?" Bess had been startled, but she felt it had been a lucky hit. Possibly Minnie had mentioned the remark to someone. The message locked in Bess's heart was known to no one else alive.

"He tells me to say, 'Rosabelle.' "

Slowly, incredibly, Bess sat up, her eyes widening. The room was disappearing. In the glow of the candlelight, time was growing fragile. Rosabelle. From their past, from their hearts.

" 'Answer,' " the voice continued. She knew it was not a command. She tried to speak, but her throat was constricted.

"B . . ." she finally managed to say.

" 'Tell.' "

There was no doubt in her mind any more.

"E . . ." she said, softly, the code, the code, how long it had taken her to learn it, all those days of practice, all those years ago, her mind still retained it somewhere in its recesses, the code they hadn't used in this century was still there when it was needed.

"Pray-answer." The double digit, Harry had explained; "pray" stood for the number one, "answer" represented the number two, together they made the number twelve, the twelfth letter of the alphabet.

"L . . ." said Bess. He would have been proud

of me, she thought. No, he *is* proud of me. The others were looking at her, doubt clouding their faces, her belief obvious, sincere, contagious.

" 'Look,' " the voice continued.

"I . . ." she said, gently, automatically.

" 'Tell.' " Arthur Ford's eyes remained closed, in the shadows the voice issuing from his lips was growing stronger, closer, more tense.

"E . . ." said Bess. She was sitting bolt upright now, frightened, frightened almost to death. What a terrible phrase, she thought, what a terrible phrase to describe the emotion she was feeling, fear and happiness at the same time.

" 'Answer-answer,' " she was anticipating now, speaking almost simultaneously with the voice.

"V . . ." she said. And then, the final word, she and the voice together, "Tell."

"E . . ." Bess said, and that was it, "B-E-L-I-E-V-E. Believe."

"He wants to know," the voice was saying, "he wants to know, 'Is this the message we agreed on, the message you wanted to hear?' "

"Yes, darling." She wasn't speaking to the voice any more, she was talking directly to him. " 'Rosabelle, believe.' I do. I do."

She was close to tears. Minnie had her hand to her mouth. She knew Bess well enough to know the emotion was real. Never mind anybody else in that room; something was happening that she had to force her mind to comprehend.

"Now he's giving me the rest of it." The voice was calmer now, the tension relaxed. "He says, 'You can take the act off your finger now.' "

Bess started to smile. Who else but Harry could have known that? Slowly, she got to her feet, the pain in her ankle making her wince, but she got to her feet so everyone could see her there in the candlelight, removing the ring that had never been off her hand in all those years, because he had been embarrassed by the emotion it would have revealed.

"He says, 'It's all right to tell them what's engraved inside. I won't deny it.' "

The United Press dispatch, quoted in the New York newspapers the next day, reported, clinically: "Mrs. Houdini raised herself, painfully, and took off her ring. Inside was engraved a song which she started to sing:

> " *'Rosabelle, sweet Rosabelle,*
>    *I love you more than I can tell;*
>    *O'er me you cast a spell*
>    *I love you, my Rosabelle.'*

"On the last notes Mrs. Houdini's voice broke, but through Ford the words came through clearly from his Control:

" 'I thank you, darling. That was the first song I ever heard you sing. You sang it in our first show, remember?' "

"Overwrought, Mrs. Houdini sobbed aloud, 'Yes.' "

The newspaper report was accurate. She was sobbing, and then she tried to smile, and she said, "My God, she's crying again," and no one knew exactly what that meant, she was certain, only the two of them, and she smiled at him once more.

Reverend Ford's eyes were still closed tightly, but his own emotion was evident. The voice spoke again, triumphantly now, warmly. This was a test no longer, it was a conversation.

"He says, 'Have you learned to speak French yet?' "

Bess nodded, unable to speak. They were in Paris, he was so annoyed at her, she was trying her best, but her best was awful.

"He is smiling now. He says, 'There are eleven words in French which finish the message.' "

Slowly, Bess started for the window, the pain in her ankle forgotten as she moved without being conscious she was moving. They were all watching, under the spell of the moment. The cynicism could wait until they got outside, until the city of New York engulfed them again; right now the moment forced that suspension of disbelief that makes Theater, and Religion, and Love, possible.

Bess stepped through the drapes, opened them, and then drew them closed with a practiced gesture: "*Je tire le rideau comme ça!*" Her French still wasn't very good, she thought, through the tears.

She clapped her hands three times, and threw the curtains wide again, threw them wide to the sunshine that broke into the startled room from the blazing star out there somewhere, from the Universe.

"*Et voilà* Le Grand Houdini!" she shouted.

She half-expected to hear the crash of cymbals, the roll of drums, the brassy music of the pit orchestra. It would have been fitting.

The vaudeville was over.

Years and years later, Minnie summed it all up this way:

"Until her death, Bess never denied that this was the exact message she and Harry had agreed on, that Halloween night when he lay dying. The newspapers decided it was all a hoax, that Harry Houdini hadn't come back. Me? I believe . . . I believe the son of a bitch loved her."

# *AFTERPIECE*

~~~~~~~~~~~~~~~~~~~

THERE was a strange aftermath to the story, one that has not been concluded even today. The storm broke in the newspapers after the first accounts appeared, and all sorts of rumors were printed and circulated in an attempt to explain what had happened, so the world could more comfortably go about the business of dying.

The New York *Sun* carried the following, all the more remarkable because it was about Margery:

## THINK HOUDINI MESSAGE GENUINE

### Stafford of Scientific American and

### Mrs. Crandon Accept It as True

Support for the claim of Mrs. Beatrice Houdini that her late husband, Harry Houdini, "Master Magician and exposer of fake psychic phenomena," had succeeded in sending to her through a spiritualist medium a message prearranged before Houdini's death on October 31, 1926, came today from John W. Stafford, associate editor of the Scientific American. . . . "There is no doubt that communication was established between a living person and one dead," Mr. Stafford asserted. . . .

The weird incident in the home of Mrs. Houdini in the northern part of the city yesterday has aroused a widespread dispute. . . .

BOSTON, Jan. 9 (U.P.)—Harry Houdini in death, has furnished the world with evidence which conclusively refutes the theories which he so vigorously defended in life, said Margery, internationally renowned medium, today. Margery, who was a "friendly enemy" of the distinguished magician on the question of post mortem communication, is the wife of Dr. L. R. G. Crandon, a Boston surgeon. She told the United Press that the supposed spirit message received yesterday by Mrs. Houdini from her husband "certainly seems to be authentic.". . .

"Mrs. Houdini," she said, "was as bitterly opposed as her husband to the theory of spirit messages, and it is obvious that she, of all, would make no effort to vindicate such beliefs."

Sir Arthur Conan Doyle wrote an article for the London *Sunday Express* captioned:

## HOUDINI'S MESSAGE FROM THE GRAVE

The news came to me in a cipher cable a week or so ago, but I make it a rule to check my statements carefully, so I cabled a direct question to Mrs. Houdini: "Is

it a fact that you have received a correct pre-arranged
cipher?" Today I received a cable: "Yes. Beatrice
Houdini.". . .

Of course, there are people whom nothing will satisfy.
When they stand before the recording angel they will put
him down to be an optical delusion.

But the ordinary man can understand evidence when
he sees it, and if he accepts the fact that this lady has
received from her husband a prearranged test, then he
will have no further doubt that the personality of Harry
Houdini is still in existence and able to impinge upon
our senses.

But that was only one side of the story. The
skeptics had a field day. The most damaging story
was in the *Journal-News* of Ithaca, New York,
where Theo Weiss was touring in Harry's old act:

## HARDEEN SAYS

## KIN'S WIDOW

## IS MISLED

### Magician Now Playing at the

### Strand Declares Brother

### Never Left Pre-Arranged

### "Spirit World" Code

Mrs. Harry Houdini is a "misguided woman, easily
led, with a lust for publicity," her brother-in-law com-
mented this morning at the Ithaca Hotel, referring to her
recent claim that Houdini had communicated a pre-

arranged code to her from the "spirit world."

Hardeen, himself a magician and an implacable foe of spiritualistic "fakirs," claims to possess the real secret code which his brother Houdini arranged before his death to communicate, if such a thing were possible. . . .

Hardeen deplores what he calls the "publicity stunt" which Houdini's widow perpetrated early this week. . . .

"Harry never left a code with his widow," Hardeen declares. "All he left her was a million dollars. He knew better than to entrust such a thing to the hands of a woman who is so easily led as is Mrs. Houdini."

And then a bombshell broke. Rea Jaure charged, in the *Graphic*, that Arthur Ford had come to her apartment the night before the seance, and revealed to her the entire message he was going to deliver the following day. Ford denied it, and produced a double who swore Miss Jaure had paid him to impersonate Ford at her apartment.

It was also revealed that much earlier, Miss Jaure had tried to get Bess Houdini to collaborate with her on a series of articles on Houdini's love life, and when she refused, had sent a photographer in disguise to take her picture in the hospital, where she was recovering from influenza.

There were also charges that Bess and the Reverend Ford were planning a vaudeville act together, and this was the publicity planned to launch it.

The most interesting story was yet to come. In an article by Asa Bordages in the New York *Telegram*, Daisy White was brought into the controversy:

## DID HOUDINI GIVE
## FISH MAN'S LADY FRIEND THAT CODE
## BEFORE HE BECAME A SPOOK?

Joseph Bantino, a chivalrous fish peddler, donned his shirt with the purple stripes and sallied forth last night to aid a lady in distress at 67 Payson Avenue.

He had, he avowed, evidence clearing Mrs. Harry Houdini of faking the "spirit message" supposedly sent by her dead husband via the self-proclaimed mediumistic powers of the Rev. Arthur Ford, pastor of the First Spiritualist Church.

"You guys get me straight," he warned reporters, "I ain't after no dough, see? If you guys think that, I'm gonna lam right now. I just ain't gonna let nobody kick a lady when she's down.". . .

Bantino finally related that he had courted a girl who knew one Daisy White, herself a magician and acquaintance of Houdini, and who lives in the same apartment house as Bantino at 255 W. 58th St. . . . He has learned that she was now a confidant of the Rev. Dr. Arthur A. Ford, pastor of the First Spiritualistic Church here. It was Dr. Ford who in a trance at Mrs. Houdini's home uttered the mystic words, "Rosabelle, believe."

Little Daisy White, at Ford's apartment, admitted knowing the fish-handler slightly, but denied everything else.

They have all died now, the principals in the drama and the comedy that followed, and the truth has never been established. Perhaps it is better to let it rest, like the spirits of those we have loved, let it all rest in the world of the Unknown.

It doesn't really matter. I, too, believe the son of a bitch loved her.

## FAWCETT CREST
## BESTSELLERS